STEVE -

You Always Keep

Me Laughing, My

Friend. Enjoy 8

Todd

LIFE IN THE BONUS ROUND:

A Game Show Host's Road to Success & Fulfillment

TODD NEWTON

iUniverse, Inc.
Bloomington

Life in the Bonus Round
A Game Show Host's Road to Success & Fulfillment

iUniverse books may be ordered through booksellers or by contacting:

iUniverse
1663 Liberty Drive
Bloomington, IN 47403
www.iuniverse.com
1-800-Authors (1-800-288-4677)

ISBN: 978-1-4759-3437-3 (sc)
ISBN: 978-1-4759-3438-0 (e)
ISBN: 978-1-4759-3439-7 (dj)

Library of Congress Control Number: 2012912199

Printed in the United States of America

iUniverse rev. date: 7/18/2012

Dedicated to Mason, Kiki, and Nana. Without the three of you there would be no words to write. I love you.

TABLE OF CONTENTS

INTRODUCTION

THE BOOK YOU NOW hold in your hands was written over the course of two years. I never set out to write my memoir, though I have long been fascinated with those of others. I never assumed that the mass audience would have an interest in investing money and time in discovering more about, well, me. The characteristics of those whom we consider to be successful and fulfilled have always captivated me. I say 'and' fulfilled because it is not possible to be genuinely successful without also feeling fulfilled. The secrets to happiness that allow some individuals to walk through life with a perpetual smile are a treasure most would like to discover. What do these people know that we have yet to learn? Why do the trials and tribulations of everyday life seem to roll off of their backs like raindrops from a duck? If we are all born with feathers, I'm curious why some 'quack' louder than others.

In the past decade, I've performed and/or presented everywhere from Paris to Honolulu, from New York to LA, from Pahrump, NV, to Plantation, FL, and most towns in between. I've spent a minimum of three nights of my life in every state in America except North Dakota. This exclusion is unintentional, I assure you. There just hasn't much demand for a motivational speakin', hypnotizin' game show host in Grand Forks.

I've stayed in five star resorts on tropical islands and shared toilets with non-English speaking travelers in the hostels of Amsterdam and Buenos Aries. Wherever my travels have taken me, this book has been by my side. Hardly a single page was written while at home. Every word, every thought, every emotion originates from its own locale. What started out as simply a collection of thoughts to pass on to my children has, over time, become a labor of love that I now wish to share with many. Using Ozark mountain arithmetic, it is 50% memoir/50% self help/50% personal diary.

Just as every man knows what needs to be done to lose weight, so does he possess the innate knowledge of what it takes to get more out of life. It's not so much a case of being lost as it is being lazy. We must take it upon ourselves to leave the unacceptable version of ourselves behind and step into the shoes of the person we want and deserve to be. This is true for you, me, and the corner grocer. Sometimes all it takes is someone to point us in the right direction, wind us up, and send us on our way. That's my job. When you've had enough of not having enough, you need someone to light your fire. I'm the guy holding the matches.

The older we get the more we evolve. I'm nothing like the person I was ten years ago. Even with all of my imperfections, I am quite proud of the current me. I am no longer a young man out to prove myself to the world. I am a father, a son, an established professional, a thinker, and a humanitarian. I love my family and I care deeply about the future of my planet. I have achieved a respectable level of success in my chosen field yet still feel as if I'm just firing up the engines. I don't do drugs and have never spent a night in jail. I have a weakness for bar food and only tell the truth approximately 85 percent of the time. I did not graduate from college yet still managed to get inducted into the school's Walk of Fame. I talk too much, listen too little, and occasionally curse when it is not appropriate. I've been in eleven fistfights and won seven of them. I love the sound of a tattoo parlor and the feel of custom tailored suits. I don't believe in God but put my faith in mankind. In other words, in spite of our differences we are very much alike.

I would never attempt to convince you that my way is the only way or what has worked for me will work for everyone. Far from it. The internet is full of self help gurus who will show you how to meditate your way to wealth or sell you the ten steps to look great in a bikini. Although I undeniably have an enormous ego, I never claim to be the prettiest or most intelligent fish in the tank. I do, however, possess incredible common sense and the curiosity of a child. That's why I have written a book that shares rather than instructs. This is the kind of book I've searched for in my own quest for personal growth. As an author and a student, I write about what I know and read about what I don't. The day I stop seeking new information is the day they tag me and bag me.

I have not produced a textbook containing the meaning of life. That meaning can only come from incorporating the value of one experience into the next. If your last bite of scrambled eggs accidentally mixes with the ketchup from your hash browns and you like the way it tastes, then you now have a tool to make tomorrow's breakfast even more enjoyable than today's. 'Life In The Bonus Round' is not a guaranteed pathway to success. No such guarantee exists. Instead, it is a collection of things I have done, people I have met, and lessons I have learned that have brought me to where I now stand. It is the ketchup on my eggs.

I encourage you to absorb the pages that follow with your mind open and receptive to previously undiscovered strategies and ideas. Doing so may very well lead to uncovering nuggets of knowledge that will then become your own to use and to share. Some stories may seem outlandish and unbelievable. Others you may find easy to relate to. Whether you gain inspiration from my successes or cringe at my misfortunes, I hope my experiences unleash new ways of thinking and introduce you to new behavioral tools that bring you that much closer to your ideal self.

TODD NEWTON
NEW YORK CITY
2012

CHAPTER 1
LITTLE T

I had as many doubts as anyone else. Standing on the starting line, we're all cowards.
-Alberto Salazar

IT ALL HAS TO start somewhere. Famed marathon runner Alberto Salazar certainly knows what it's like to stand on the starting line and wait for the pistol to fire signifying the beginning of something exciting yet terrifying. You and I have had our share of beginnings, as well. And who's to say one person's beginning is any less nerve-racking than that of another? The first day of school, a new job, that first date...all cause that anxious souring of the stomach. But the beginning of life is nothing short of exhilarating. I don't mean the moment that Mom and Dad did what none of us want to picture Mom and Dad doing. I mean being a kid and learning to do the things that, as adults, we often take for granted. This is not limited to reading, writing, and speaking. Most go on to pick those things up eventually and at their own pace. I'm focusing more on the skills needed for survival and happiness. Things like patience, tolerance, communication, respect, ambition, health, and love. Sadly, these subjects aren't outlined in textbooks and you won't receive college credit for showing compassion to another, but they are learned through experiences like taking a punch, getting dumped by your first girlfriend, and falling off your bicycle. Salazar is right, we are all cowards before we take that first step because we have no experience to show us how to arrive safely at the finish line. We have no possible way of knowing what we may encounter between Point A and Point B. But, if you think about it, would you really want it any other way? In some ways the beginning is just as exciting as the end.

I was born May 5th, 1970, in St. Louis. I love my hometown. It gives you a little bit of everything. You'll find the razzle dazzle of the big city with just enough Ozark backwoods hillbilly mixed in to keep it honest. We were an upper middle class family. My parents still live in the home I grew up in. It's your standard two story house located in a subdivision in a nice suburb known as Oakville. The walls are filled with pictures of my brother and me in every stage of life. The basement is jam packed with toys and old clothes with too much sentimental value to be thrown away. The smell of potpourri gives it that extra "homey" feel just as it did when I was a kid. Mom still sets the supper table every night around five o'clock. She's one of four people I've heard actually use the word 'supper.' The good things never change.

Sidewalks out front always made for safe bike riding and an easy path to our friends' houses after school. Dad put up a basketball hoop in the driveway so I could practice my free throws and our fenced in backyard was perfect for playing catch. It was the contemporary version of a Norman Rockwell painting.

Jim Newton first saw Anne Kruse rollerskating in the rec center at Tower Grove Baptist Church. Jim was the jock and Anne was the cute little cheerleader with the cat eye glasses. Their courtship was an innocent and respectful one that eventually led to marriage and the birth of two sons. My brother Jarrod is four years younger than I am and just about anyone will tell you that we could not be more opposite. Many have said over the years that he got the IQ and I got the EQ-which translates to he's the smart one and I'm the loud one. Jarrod is the kind of guy who reserves his words for the opportune moment, whereas I will spout off about anything at anytime. He was the skinny kid while I was the chubby one. He chose to build a life for himself in our home state of Missouri and I chose to pack my bags and head for the bright lights of Hollyweird. Growing up we argued, fought, spit, cussed, and then hugged it out the way siblings always do. We're night and day, oil and vinegar, peanut butter and toothpaste, but I love the guy.

I was into all of the typical things as a boy. Sports, riding my bike with my friends, flirting with girls, causing a little trouble around the neighborhood, cheeseburgers, and thinking of ways to make money. I also loved to read. As I've mentioned, I have always seemed to gravitate toward biographies and autobiographies. I enjoy hearing about where others have come from and how they got to be where they are. Even as a young boy I saw that good old fashioned trial and error is one of the most effective forms of learning and there is much to be gained from the mistakes made by those who have come before us. I never saw the sense in touching a hot stove twice. As an adult, what I'm constantly astounded by in these books is how many people have had such eventful childhoods. Tragic accidents, absentee parents, homelessness, poverty, and so on. Authoring a book is, in its own way, a form of show business so I have to believe there is a certain degree of fabrication involved in some of these writings. I salute anyone who overcomes any sort of adversity and achieves happiness, but it seems impossible that some featured in these books would have any shot at a normal life whatsoever given the hundreds of pages of misery they publish. In comparison to many, my early years were quite vanilla. My mom and dad loved us and taught us the difference between right and wrong. We went to a Baptist church. I got decent grades in school and, for the most part, I kept my nose clean.

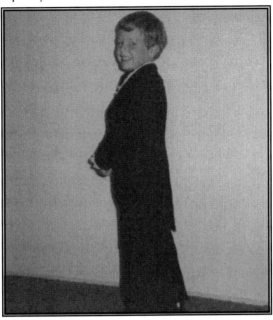

The first of many tuxedos. 1976.

I don't get back to St. Louis nearly as often as I'd like, but when I am able to I prefer to spend a night or two at my parents' house. These visits provide us with some quality time together and allow me to rummage through boxes of junk that they've held onto and stored in my former bedroom. On a recent trip to Lisbon, Portugal, I was introduced to a word that matches my feelings for home. The Lisboans use the term *saudade* to describe a heightened passion for the past. I experience *saudade* as I look through old pictures, walk around the old neighborhood, and listen to family stories. I also relish in the nostalgia that can only come from lying in my childhood bed and envisioning the Magic Johnson and Cheryl Tiegs posters that used to adorn those walls. It's hard to believe they are the same four walls that surrounded me while I pondered the universe and worked my way through everything a young boy must work through while becoming a man. If those walls could talk I doubt they would say anything that would be of much interest to anyone but me, but we all need to return to our roots from time to time and get back to basics. That room will always be my safe, happy place. It is also where my entrepreneurial spirit was born.

I was six years old when I came to the realization that the more money I had the more baseball cards I could buy. I collected every player in the league every season at a time when you couldn't just run down to your local Target and buy the whole series in one swoop for $50. It was a hobby, a challenge, and a great feeling of accomplishment when I'd finally come across that elusive Clint Hurdle card that rounded out the '76 Kansas City Royals. But I soon discovered that my little past time could get pricey.

Sometimes the best things in life aren't free at all. I found that I needed to put a little jingle in my pocket if I was going to enjoy all the fine things a boy needs to enjoy. With the help of my childhood buddy, and Big Wheel riding partner, Tony Shuman, I set out on a money making venture that would be a clear indication of the path my life would take.

Our business plan was quite simple- we would go door to door and tell jokes for a dime. Together, we collected old garage sale and lost puppy signs made of poster board, turned them over, and wrote **Jokes 10 cents** on the back with thick, black markers. Not the most strategic marketing plan, I'll admit, but it would serve the purpose. Dressed in matching Hawaiian shirts, we'd parade up and down the street ringing doorbells and bringing smiles to the faces of our neighbors by offering comedic value the likes of which they'd never seen.

"Have ya heard the joke about the bed? It hasn't been made yet. Get it?"

"Have ya heard the one about the rope? Ah…just skip it. Get it?

It wasn't until I was in my early thirties that a comic buddy of mine told me I should stop asking people if they get the punchline at the end of all of my jokes.

"If you have to ask then your material stinks," he'd say.

There's no question many of the dimes we collected were given just to get rid of us or because they thought we were cute, but a dime is a dime and we weren't complaining. Tony was the straight man while I was the cut up. The Abbott to my Costello. We were a hit…pulling in at least a buck a day. Sometimes Tony and I would laugh harder amongst ourselves than our paying customers did. We bought so many baseball cards that we would put our double and triple copies in the spokes of our bicycle wheels. We had a good run but the well of material soon ran dry. After pulling every last riddle, limerick, and one liner out of our children's joke books, our act eventually faded into the dusty hallows of great comedy teams of yore. But from those corny jokes a young self promoter was born.

The times spent playing with Tony were great ones, but not every memory brings back such warm and fuzzy feelings. As adults we all have that one childhood recollection sure to make us cringe when we think about it. It is that one incident that, if given the opportunity by a Barbara Eden-esque genie, we'd eliminate from our life story without a moment's hesitation. Rather than erase it, however, I choose to share it in hopes that from my tragedy comes a bit of comedy. Unfortunately, I didn't collect any dimes from this one.

Ms. Merkel was my 1st grade teacher. Our classroom was the stereotypical four walls filled with restless students at desks and the smell of a dusty chalkboard ever present in the air. Once every couple of weeks the bookmobile, a library on wheels, would visit our school. The bookmobile had a fraction of the books our regular library had but it was a nice break from the routine and we all saw it as a special treat.

More so than the other kids, I could not wait for these visits. Only the bookmobile carried a series of books highlighting all of my favorite monsters from movies I wasn't allowed to watch. There was a book on Dracula, another on the Mummy, Frankenstein, etc. I had read them all except for one, the Wolfman. It was always checked out and I'd have to settle for rereading one of the others or grabbing the latest Hardy Boys mystery.

Visit after visit I would scan the shelves only be disappointed by its absence. I had nearly come to terms with the fact that my fascination with transmogrification (look it up) would go unfed until, one day, my luck changed. As the girls in my class wrestled the latest Judy Blume novel out of each others fingers, I made a direct line for where I knew my desired work of literary horror was to be located. Sure enough, there it was. The Wolfman, with a fang-filled snarl, was glaring at me from the cover of the book that I was beginning to think may have been hijacked by some greedy kid from another school. I grabbed it and took my place at the end of a long line. One by one the kids in front of me handed their library cards to the librarian.

She was a sweet woman who loved to chit chat with us and never seemed to be in any sort of a hurry. As a result, checking out could often be a painstakingly slow process. As I patiently waited my turn, I started to feel that all too familiar sting originating from my bladder. What was just the initial feeling of having to use the little boy's room got progressively more intense the longer I had to wait. And the longer I had to wait the more I thought about having to go. The more I thought about having to go the slower the line seemed to be moving. Suddenly

5

I found myself with a serious decision to make. We weren't allowed to take books out without seeing the librarian first and she would not hold books for us. She'd explained many times there were just too many kids still to visit the bookmobile for her to reserve books. It had come down to a now or never, game time situation. I either had to put the book back on the shelf and hope it would be there when I returned or continue standing in line and hope for the best. I had to choose...now. I chose to hope for the best...but sometimes the best evades us.

I remember thinking, "This can't be happening." Wetting one's pants is a surreal experience. That split second where your body takes over your mind and just lets things happen feels as if it must be happening to someone else. It's not until you feel the warmth soaking the crotch of your pants and running down your leg that you fully come to terms with the fact that you're pissing yourself. Sadly for me, the floodgates had been lifted.

I tossed the book on the nearest shelf and dashed out of the bookmobile before a puddle could form at my feet. As I hurdled the steps, I plowed into a classmate named George Boswell. George and I didn't really get along and I had no intention of sharing the details of my current situation with him. I was in full survival mode and used the impact from our collision to propel myself further away from the other kids.

The nearest entrance to the school led into the cafeteria. Lunchtime was over so everyone had left except for the playground attendant, Mrs. Mazak. She was a strict, no nonsense disciplinarian but had always been very sweet to me. Plus, I had no one else to turn to for help. She assessed the situation and, like a Secret Service agent protecting the integrity of the President, ushered me to the nurse's office at a brisk pace, stepping in front of me when we'd encounter someone in the hall.

I guess there aren't many things an elementary school nurse hasn't seen. Banged up knees and pencil erasers stuck in nostrils prepare you for just about any crisis. Our nurse didn't seem the least bit shocked when I appeared before her soaked in urine. She instructed me to take off my pants as she very casually walked over to a large wooden crate that held lost and found items. As I stood there in nothing but my tightie whities, she pulled out a pair of brown corduroy pants and handed them to me. They were hideous looking and far from a perfect fit but they would have to do the trick. As curious as I was, I certainly was in no position to ask how some boy lost his pants at school so I just kept my mouth shut and slipped them on. She tossed my wet jeans into a plastic bag and told me to come by on my way home to pick them up. Catastrophe averted. I was home free...or so I thought.

Mrs. Mazak walked me back to the bookmobile to retrieve the Wolfman book. Thankfully it was still there. I'd hate to think my traumatic experience had been suffered in vain. I felt like skipping as I made my way to the classroom. I really felt as if I'd gotten away with the perfect crime. Ms. Merkel always gave us some time to read our new books after a bookmobile visit. Like the rest of my classmates, I was quietly thumbing through page after page, absorbing every picture, when the piercing voice of George Boswell broke the peaceful silence...

"Todd Newton pee'd his pants in the bookmobile!"

He might as well have said it through a bullhorn. The snickers of my classmates were quickly hushed by our teacher but the damage had already been done. I could feel my face turning fire engine red with humiliation. I know how tough it is to completely bomb on stage in front of an audience. This was a hundred times worse. What was probably sixty seconds seemed like sixty minutes until finally everyone reconnected with their books and the moment passed. To my benefit, kids have short attention spans and, other than a few taunts at recess, nothing really came of it. The nurse really saved me with those used britches, but what George Boswell did is still burned on my brain.

I learned a long time ago that sometimes you have to let things go, but there was definitely a time when George was number one on my list. Kids can be brutal. It's as if they have no filter. At age seven no one would have blamed me if I'd popped him right in the nose out on the playground, but I knew better. We are faced with situations throughout our lives where the initial reaction is to retaliate physically in order to save face or seek revenge. It's never the right decision no matter how strong that carnal, animalistic urge may be. I have been in my share of scraps over the years but have never once felt good about it afterwards. I'm thankful for the lesson learned that day, but saddened by the fact I'm stuck with a lifelong aversion to corduroy pants as a result of it.

As a youngster I was what blue jean manufacturers call "husky." I wouldn't consider myself fat per se, but I definitely carried a few extra pounds around with me during my early years. My weight never really bothered me until 5th or 6th grade when, coincidentally, is also when I started to pay more attention to girls. This is the age when boys and girls begin to come together on the playground and conversations begin to have a little substance. What used to be complete avoidance of one another just a few months prior now has morphed into complete fascination. I saw who the girls were paying attention to and it wasn't me as often as I would have liked for it to have been.

I was too young to consciously attempt to be funny in order to get girls to like me. My nature is to see the comedy in any given situation and it didn't take long for other kids to realize that where Todd was, good times weren't far away. I had the ability to make people laugh and that always made me feel good. The young ladies weren't exactly swooning over me, but they always sat next to me in the cafeteria and that counted for something.

My parents were always very active in the community and, looking back, I realize how much this meant to me as well as to so many others. My father, and his father before him, was very athletic. He still is to a certain degree. He officiated high school and college baseball and basketball games in addition to his full time job. He didn't do it for the money. It was so he could be out there with the athletes feeling the heat and working the hustle. He loves the competitiveness and sportsmanship. I can still remember the sight of his dust covered umpire gear in the trunk of his car. One of the chores he used to give me was bringing it all into the garage after his games. Sometimes, just for fun, I'd strap on the chest protector and slip on his face mask. I recall now how big it all felt as it hung off my young body.

He also played fast pitch softball in our church league. I would volunteer to be the bat boy so I could stand close to the field and watch him pitch. It blew my mind how fast he could throw that ball. "Rock 'n Fire, Jim!" is what his teammates would yell from the field. I loved the whizzing sound the ball would make before it popped into the glove of the catcher. My dad was the quintessential guy's guy and he parlayed his love of sports into an endeavor that would benefit many.

When I was in junior high school, my father started a youth basketball organization called the Patriots. It began as just two teams, one my age and a younger team for my brother's age group. Initially, the team was made up of me and my friends and we would play other teams from churches and schools throughout the St. Louis area. My dad had a lot of contacts and our seasons often consisted of thirty or more games.

Each year, more and more guys would want to try out for the team. In addition to learning the fundamentals of basketball and teamwork, the Patriots stood for being a model citizen, staying away from drugs and alcohol, and focusing on your schoolwork. Integrity and responsibility were big. If you screwed up at home or in school you didn't play. Period. This was the ideal way to teach (and learn) accountability and respect. I'm certain this is a large part of the reason I never chose to use drugs. In order to be the man I want to be for my family and for my career I need to maintain a clear head and a clear heart. Drugs, alcohol, and cigarettes don't play into that. I thank my father for instilling that within me from an early age.

By the time I hit the 8th grade being a Patriot really meant something. My teammates and I would parade around school in our red team jackets and the girls all wanted to be cheerleaders-which my mom took upon herself to organize and oversee. Now, let me speak on that for a moment. When your mother is the head of cheerleading, and every girl your age wants to *be* a cheerleader, that puts you in a pretty admirable position. The word *leverage* comes to mind. The girls were constantly calling our house to ask about tryouts or practices and I made sure I was the one to answer the phone. We'd chit chat for a minute or two and then I would give them the info they were seeking. Before letting the young lady go, I'd always try and throw something witty in just to make sure she was giggling when she hung up. I loved making girls laugh. It established rapport and while other guys were working every trick in the book to get a girl's phone number, all I had to do was sit back and wait. My phone rang more than a Chinese takeout joint.

My dad did something really cool at the beginning of my freshman year in high school. He began to enter the Patriots in tournaments outside of St. Louis which meant we would go on two or three road trips each season. A few of the guys left our team to play for the school, but for the most part it was the same group year after year. By this point we were like brothers. Our team was pretty good and we were having a blast just being young and cocky.

I'd had a growth spurt during the summer and entered high school a taller, leaner, and even more confident (if you can believe it) Todd. There was one guy on our team that had even more confidence than I did, and he had every right to. My buddy Marc was the only one out of all of us who had had sex. He never really talked about it, which only led to us coming to our own conclusions about how mind blowing of an experience it must be. His girlfriend's name was Sue and they had been together for what seemed like forever. They were *the* couple. Sue was, and still is, beautiful with an outgoing personality and a radiant smile. They were popular when being popular was considered to be important. Naturally, the entire school was shocked when they eventually broke up.

Almost immediately, Sue started seeing our buddy Dan. As men get older it becomes sort of taboo for a guy to date the ex of one of his friends, but in your early teens those guidelines have yet to be established. Sue and Dan were not a good fit for each other. I remember being at Dan's house one afternoon and watching the two of them make out on the couch. They both had their eyes wide open and I couldn't help but bust out laughing. Sexy it definitely was not. They didn't last long.

We were on a ball trip in Memphis one weekend and I ran into Sue at the hotel soda machine. Kids were roaming all around the hotel. Some were in the arcade, some by the pool, others hanging out in their rooms. Sue and I decided to take a walk together. We were good friends and always had plenty to talk about, but Sue had something on her mind that night. We eventually found ourselves in a little rock garden leading to the indoor pool area. I can still remember the smell of chlorine burning the inside of my nostrils. Sue pulled me into a corner and kissed me. I'd only kissed a couple of girls at this point and neither of them had been anything to write about in my diary. Sue was another story. She knew how to kiss! Sue was the one who lit me up. She was in charge and I was more than happy to go with it. When she finally pulled away (I had no concept of time so can't even begin to tell you how long that kiss lasted) she whispered a phrase into my ear that I will never forget...

"I want to make love to you."

I couldn't breathe. Seriously. All the blood in my body immediately shot to one region and I became dizzy. I would love to be able to share my response with you but, for the life of me, cannot begin to remember how I reacted. To be honest, I wouldn't be surprised if it was something along the lines of, "Yes, please."

Then, as now, I recognized an opportunity when I saw one and began thinking of places Sue and I could sneak off to. Keep in mind that all of our friends, and my parents, were lurking about. This had to be done undercover. There were four kids to a room so that was out. The bus was locked so that was out. Location, or a lack thereof, eventually became the ultimate blocker and, much to my grave disappointment, I was not able to become a man on that warm Memphis evening. The adolescent passion quickly faded for both of us when we returned home and to school. It was only meant to be that one night and we slipped back into friendship mode. Looking back, I can truthfully say that I probably wasn't ready anyway.

My parents threw a little party for me before I left for Los Angeles in 1995 and Sue came by. Out on the back deck we talked and laughed about that night so many years ago. Sue, now married with three beautiful kids, gave me a little kiss on my cheek and wished me luck. That little peck from a longtime friend meant even more to me than the teenage spit swap in Tennessee

There was a Patriot team a year below us and they would often come along when we hit the road. An eighth grade team meant there were also eighth grade cheerleaders. I had never really paid much attention to any of the girls on the younger squad. When you're fourteen years old you're really only focused on girls that are older than you. But I was soon to discover, on a trip to Louisville, KY, that the younger girls were not to be ignored.

The bus was packed. With two teams, two sets of cheerleaders, and all the chaperones, there was not an empty seat to be had. Somehow I ended up sitting next to an eighth grade girl named Beth. She was cute and I began to think this might be worth exploring. The music was so loud and there was so much talking on the bus that it was difficult to have a real conversation. Not that I had any pertinent topics I wished to discuss with her. Politics, stem cell research, stopping genocide...these weren't things that came up very often at that age. Mainly we talked about our favorite videos on MTV and why Boy George dressed the way he did. The ride suddenly took a turn for the better when Beth's friend Kelly came and sat with us. Suddenly there was plenty to talk about. Kelly was a stunner! I couldn't believe I had never noticed her before. A beautiful brunette with big, brown eyes...and quite developed for a girl her age. And just like that (as is often the case when it comes to attraction) Louisville had a purpose.

I brought out my funniest material, sat with her during food stops, showed off for her during the games, and made sure all of her friends knew I was interested so I would be the topic of their slumber party chats. Eventually I got up the nerve to ask her to go out with me. This was no small feat. To a young man, the risk of being rejected by a girl you've really got a thing for is enough to make you run for the hills and I had never been out on an official date before. But, as Wayne Gretzky once said, "You miss a hundred percent of the shots you don't take," so I had to go for it. I wouldn't exactly say courage was the motivator. The desire was more hormonal than anything, but you use what you've got.

My mother had a list with all of the cheerleaders numbers on it and kept it right next to our phone. One night, when I could steal a little privacy, I called Kelly's number and she answered. This was 1985 and the hot, new phone feature was call waiting. Everyone who was anyone had it and, with the new beep that let you know someone else was trying to reach you, busy signals had pretty much become a thing of the past. This meant that if Kelly was home I would get to speak to her.

There was definitely that initial urge to hang up when I heard her voice but I was able to push through it. She seemed somewhat surprised to hear from me even though word had gotten around that I was looking to get her attention. Since I was a year older I needed to keep my cool and pretend that calling girls out of the blue was nothing new for me. After a bit of small talk I finally got around to asking her out for that Friday night. She said she would ask her parents and call me back. Normally this would have thrown me for a loop but since her folks, actually *everyone's* folks, knew and liked my parents I was confident we'd get the go ahead.

Tony Dudash, a friend and teammate of mine, was a year or two older than the rest of us. Tony had an AMC Pacer at the time and agreed to drive if he and his girlfriend could come along. If you're not familiar with what a Pacer is (or was), please don't consider yourself shortchanged. It was a hideous little compact vehicle that looked like something the Jetsons would sell for scrap. As a matter of fact, *World Auto News & Reviews* gave it the number one spot on The Most Idiotic Cars Of All Time list. No one was sure how old Dudash really was. He was that guy, and every school has one, that obviously had been held back. It was just that none of us knew how many times. Didn't matter. He's the one that turned me on to Bob Seger and he had wheels. Our twosome had just become a foursome.

The four of us stood at the box office and collectively chose to see a movie called *Iron Eagle*. We grabbed popcorn, sodas, and Junior Mints before making our way to four seats in the very last row of the theater.

Midway through the flick I reached out and took Kelly's hand in mine. It was beautiful. Just as meeting rejection would have set me back a few steps, her little signs of acceptance boosted my confidence. I felt so comfortable with her. Without even trying, she had calmed me. She was beautiful, funny, and we both had braces. A match made in orthodontic heaven.

After the movie we grabbed a quick bite at a small, inexpensive Italian eatery before taking Kelly home. She had a curfew and I had run out of money so calling it a night seemed like the right thing to do. In one of the smoothest wingman moves in the history of first dates, Tony parked down the street so I could walk Kelly to her door without being watched. There's really no way to describe that moment when you really want to kiss a girl but have no idea if she wants to kiss you.

Some women will make it pretty clear that you've got a green light but many keep their cards close to their chest and make you work for it. I've grown to like working for it. Easy isn't my thing.

Kelly thanked me for a nice evening and gave me a hug. As we began to pull away I just went for it. Our lips touched and our first kiss was set into motion. It was amazing. First kisses with someone you genuinely have feelings for generally are. It's as if your body and mind come together in a massive explosion of endorphins and adrenaline. There's no way to explain it. She smiled at me, walked inside, and closed the door.

As I made my way back to Tony's Pacer, I noticed the smell of the flowers in her yard. I have no idea what kind they were, but I've encountered that particular aroma here and there throughout my adult life and it always puts a nostalgic smile on my face.

Kelly and I dated all throughout high school. We laughed and cried together. We battled through our formative years together so it's no wonder that she was my "first."

Having a steady girlfriend when you're young is really the way to go. I'm not a huge advocate of "til death do us part." It seems unnatural and a tad macabre to me. Nevertheless, when you're in that exploratory stage of life it's nice to have someone who is just as inexperienced and curious about the ways of the world as you are. Neither one of us had any idea what we were doing until we did it with each other. One thing would naturally lead to another until there was really only one thing left for us to do.

My father was good about filling me in on the birds and the bees. I think I was in fifth grade when we had that special bonding moment and it was only spurred by my asking him at the dinner table if he knew what "screwing" meant.

As my entire family choked on their Sloppy Joe sandwiches, I explained it's when the guy sticks his wiener in the girl and spins around. It was straight up to my room we marched. My father's definition of the act was slightly more clinical and incredibly more awkward. The films they showed us in Health class were only good for a few chuckles every time the voiceover guy said the word 'testicles.' Let's face it, when it comes to the deed itself, we all just kick into autopilot and hope we don't injure ourselves.

Kelly and I both knew the day was coming when we'd finally take that big step. Two teenagers can only steam up so many car windows before they self implode. We had several spots where we liked to park and would often spend two or three hours lovin', touchin', and squeezin' each other until we couldn't take it anymore.

At school, we would pass each other notes between every class. Normally they consisted of little more than who said what but I nearly fell out of my chair when, one morning, she wrote that her parents were going out of town that weekend and leaving her home alone. Constantly wondering what sex is like is one thing. Knowing you're going to find out in a matter of days is another. I was about to step up into the big leagues. We talked about it at lunch that day and agreed that it would probably be best if my parents didn't know about her parents' leaving town. That would only put them on high alert. We just remained casual and never let on to any of our friends that anything was out of the ordinary for fear of it getting back to my folks. I'm normally pretty good at keeping a secret but holding this kind of information back from my buddies was torture. If there was ever a time to puff my chest out and do some bragging this was it. But loose lips sink ships and I didn't want to rock this boat in the least.

That Friday night Kelly was going to be cheerleading at a hockey game. I never missed a chance to see her in that outfit. Before making my way to the ice rink, I stopped by Walgreen's to pick up gum, a soda, and some protection. We rarely acknowledge how unnerving it is to be young and shopping for prophylactics in a well lit drugstore half a mile from your home. You feel as if you are walking under a spotlight and every person in the store is holding their breath to see if you go for lubricated or non-lubricated.

After five minutes of feeling as if I was on display, I panicked and grabbed the first box I saw. A three pack of Trojans. In hindsight I would have purchased them days earlier so I could do a few practice runs, but obviously I had other topics on my mind. Those things are slippery and not easy to get on at first. The directions provided in the box sure don't help. Raise your hand if you've ever put a condom on backwards! See? We are not alone. A couple of rehearsals, or perhaps a big red dot indicating which side is up, would have come in pretty handy.

I was voted "Best Sense of Humor" in my senior class but had been resorting to cracking jokes in order lighten an uncomfortable situation for as long as I could remember. I was more nervous than a whore in church when the big night arrived. I'm sure Kelly was, as well. Throughout the hockey game I would casually wave the light blue box of condoms in the air so only she could see it. This would make her laugh and it helped pass the time until we could get out of there and get on with it already.

Admittedly, there was a part of me that just wanted the whole thing to be over with and for us to be holding each other tenderly on the other side of it. I'm often guilty of setting my expectations too high, but I really wanted it to be perfect for both of us. It was important to me that Kelly enjoy it and, more importantly, that she feel good about it after. Losing your virginity as a boy is a huge deal. Having a girl give you *her* virginity is monumental. We were both glad we were doing it at the same time...and with each other. As far as being "right" goes, this was about as close to perfect as we were going to get.

We didn't even turn the lights on when we got into her house. We went straight to her bedroom and took off our clothes. Our bodies were nothing new to each other but the emotions we were feeling certainly were. Time seemed to be moving in slow motion. We were doing what two kids in love do. We took it slow and savored each moment of the beautiful chaos. The first time is never pleasant for the woman, or so I've heard them say on *The View*. But for me it was incredible.

It's indescribable. It's almost like an out of body experience when the physical pleasure blasts through your preconceived notions and leaves you panting in disbelief. I've never done hard drugs but no one could ever convince me there's a substance that can make me feel as good as I did right then. I can't say how it was for Kelly, and I was too young and caught up in the moment to think to ask, but she didn't cry or throw me out. A man should always take that as a good sign.

We had nowhere we had to be and nothing we had to say. It was all about the silence. Life had now changed for both of us and we'd gotten one step closer to being the adults we already thought we were.

There we were, holding each other under the covers, two young lovers enjoying the sweet, pure afterglow when suddenly...*Ding Dong*!

The ringing of the doorbell instantly brought us back down to Earth. We both sat up in complete shock. It was almost midnight and she was supposedly home alone. I got out of bed, still naked, and walked to her bedroom window which overlooked the front porch. There was only one person in the world who could have caused the shrinkage I experienced when I pulled back the curtain...my mother.

It was no use pretending. My car was parked in the street and she obviously knew Kelly's parents were out of town. Kelly had purchased a white, lace neglige for our special night. Apparently her parents had discovered it and decided it might be wise to let my folks know they would be away. Parents have a way of putting two and two together and Mom had decided to swing by. I'm sure my father was at home laughing his tail off, but my God fearing mother was none to pleased that we were alone in a dark house late at night.

We both managed to throw our clothes on in the time it took to get to the front door. She walked in, eyed us suspiciously, and told me it was time to get home. Although there's no way of knowing if she knew what we were up to, I felt as if she had been right in Kelly's bedroom and witnessed everything. As my mother walked back to her car I hugged Kelly and told her that I loved her. Not exactly a fairytale ending, but an unforgettable night nonetheless. Today love means something altogether different to me, but back then, looking into those brown eyes, I meant it with every ounce of my being.

I don't know where Kelly is today. I've heard she got married and my guess is she probably has a baby or four. I hope life has been kind and that she, on that rare occasion when she smells the flowers by her old front door, thinks back to our time together and smiles. You only get one "first."

Every little boy and girl deserves a childhood they can look back on fondly. Sadly, we don't all begin on the same starting line and some have higher hurdles to jump than others. As parents, it's our duty to do everything in our power to give our children a better life than the one we had. I made a promise to both of my kids the moment they were born that I would always be here for them. Not only as a protector and provider, but as a father who will love, support, and guide them as best I can. More than anything, our kids need to know that they are not alone. They don't always act as if they want us around, but deep down they most definitely do. They deserve to know that they are loved and that they are unique. It is a parent's responsibility to let kids know, even though it's not always easy, that things somehow have a way of working out for the best. Childhood is more than trips to the circus and cookies at Grandma's house. It's bumps and bruises. It's falling off your bike. It's wetting your pants in the bookmobile.

*Ready to take on the world! With Mom and Dad
on Graduation Day. 1988.*

We cannot always control what happens to us. We can, however, control our physical and emotional responses. This knowledge is an incredible gift to give to a child. Acquiring the power to control our outcomes requires discipline and, fortunately, can be learned early on. It is discovered through even the smallest and seemingly most meaningless of experiences. No matter how old we become, we never stop learning how to adapt and embrace change. Life is full of unknowns and, regardless of how or where yours may have begun, it is far from over.

I am beyond grateful for the life my parents gave me. Not only in terms of material things. They let me be a kid. My brother and I always knew our mom would be there after school and that our dad would make sure there was food on the table. We knew if we got out of line we'd be put right back in place. I never once questioned whether or not my parents supported me or my dreams. We had grandparents that spoiled us rotten because that's what good grandparents do. Today, my kids have all of those things and more. My son has been written up for talking in class and my daughter has been tossed from a horse during a riding lesson. From these experiences lessons have been learned. Lessons that will stay with them forever. It's just part of being a kid. It's part of the beginning.

CHAPTER 2
THE GREATEST WIFFLE BALL
PITCHER IN THE WORLD

Grandma always made you feel she had been waiting to see just you all day and now the day was complete.
- Marcee DeMaree

I'M NEVER GOING TO make it through this chapter without crying. I'm putting that on the table right up front. Closing my eyes and picturing my Nana destroys me every single time. If I was a leading man on a soap opera and needed to shed a tear in a scene where I had just been told my estranged brother had escaped from prison ten years ago, made love to my wife who had passed away in a tragic lawn mowing accident, and was the real father of the twins I never knew I had, I would think of Nana and instantly be ready for my close-up.

Some memories are planted so deeply within us that we know they will be crystal clear in our minds forever. Honestly, I can't even remember what the last movie I saw was but I can remember playing wiffle ball with my brother and Nana in her backyard as if I just came in from outside to get a drink of water. I guess if I were sitting in a shrink's office and she asked me about my fondest childhood memories, watching Nana smile as she pitched underhand to me would top the list.

Everyone, especially children, needs people around them who are not only positive influences but who love them. I mean *really* love them. Unconditionally. When we become adults our needs obviously change and we need friends, mentors, lovers, coaches, and a good attorney. But as children all we need are people who are going to keep us from killing ourselves by sticking keys in an electrical outlet, people that will make sure there is food on the table that will nourish our bodies, people to teach us right from wrong, and people who make us feel loved.

I, of course, had my parents who love me to no end. But I also had the winning lottery ticket...I had Nana.

*Nana taught me to enjoy the good things in life, like
warm chocolate chip cookies and cold milk.*

Eleanor Roseman was born in the great city of St. Louis, MO, on
Friday, May 16, 1920. We are both Taurus'. I think zodiac signs and the
vague, generalized personality traits that are associated with them are
completely meaningless, but I do think it's cool she and I have that in
common.

Shortly after her birth, the Roseman family moved to the small
town of Newburg, MO, where her father, Louis, took a job as a railroad
detective. I've only seen one, very old and very faded photograph of
Louis, but he looked like a tough son of a bitch. He had to be in order
to keep the bums off of those railroad cars. Judging from the stories
Nana used to tell, he was pretty much the Dog the Bounty Hunter of
his day. A real rough and tumbler with a heart of gold. He seemed to
be able to look past first impressions and see the real person inside.
This is a characteristic I am working on for myself. When I'm hosting a
show, I can look at a contestant and instantly know there's something
beautiful and special about that individual that the audience needs to
see and I will keep digging until it is revealed. I'm not always that way
in everyday life. Rub me the wrong way at the get go and the get go
becomes get gone. Louis wasn't like that. He understood that the reason
a man is risking his life by running alongside an empty freight car in
the middle of the night is because he really needs to get somewhere
and he doesn't have the money for a ticket. Maybe he needed a lift to
Kansas City so he could find a job to support his family. Maybe he was

trying to get back home. Maybe he just needed a fresh start in new town. He knew, as I know, that people are generally good. He just had more patience than I do.

According to Nana, it was not uncommon for Big Lou to go as far as to invite the occasional stowaway home to have dinner with his family. My memories of Nana's mother are few. Nannie is what I called her and what my kids now call my mother. I do recall that she spent a lot of time in the kitchen when we would visit her home in Memphis so I'm certain these home cooked meals were like hitting the mother load for a man living out on the tracks.

The humanitarian in me finds these stories to be beautiful. What a magnificent heart he, and the whole family, must have had to welcome a complete stranger into their home and share a meal. I can only imagine how fascinating the conversations must have been. This hobo sharing his tales of life on the rails and the kids listening with wide eyed wonder. I can't think of a better example of generosity and love for your fellow man than that displayed by Big Lou and his wife.

Now, the father in me thinks bringing a homeless man home is just nucking futs...and that's not a typo. Just the other day, my kids and I encountered a real looney bird in full Central Casting crazy fashion and I kicked into full papa bear mode to make sure there was a football field worth of space between him and my kids. I'm especially protective of my daughter but I don't let any suspicious characters anywhere near either one of them. The Roseman's had four daughters and all of them were, as odd as this is to say about family, drop dead gorgeous. In order of age they were Rue, Kay, Nana, and Barb.

As a boy growing up I used to get very excited when the house next door or across the street would go up for sale. I'd hope against hope that a family with a bevy of beautiful daughters would move in and turn my life into one unforgettable 80's teen flick. You know, watching the girls sunbathe, having one of them flick her lights on and off when it was safe for me to climb in her bedroom window, watching them spray each other with the garden hose as they washed the car...that kind of thing. Every boy has the same dream at some point. Some lucky kid in Newburg actually got to live it.

There are times when generosity can turn around and bite you. It's happened to all of us. When it does, it only serves to add another layer to our armor and make us less likely to open our hearts and wallets the next time around. It's unfortunate, but *Once Bitten Twice Shy* is more than just a tune by the band Great White. It's actually a natural reaction and proven defense mechanism against being taken advantage of. As a result, the older we get the more calloused we become.

Having a heart of gold eventually came back to haunt Big Lou when a bum he threw off a train became so irate that he threatened to seek revenge on the family. The details are a bit sketchy to me because, as she told the story, Nana would whisper so my brother and I wouldn't overhear. Being the curious cat that I am, I forced myself to read her lips. I have also taken the liberty to fill in a few of the blanks with how I imagine the tale probably unfolded.

This drifter was no stranger to Big Lou, and I'm sure Big Lou was no stranger to any of the bums. In fact, I believe he was somewhat of a legend that they tried to steer as clear from as possible. The man stood as tall as a mighty oak and had paws like a catcher's mitt. Safe to assume Big Lou may have even had this particular fella home for one of Nannie's famous meatloaf dinners.

One evening during a routine patrol, he uncovered the man tucked away behind some wooden crates in the corner of a freight car. After a short struggle, Lou pulled him out and sent him on his way. In that classic detective show style, the stowaway shook his fist in anger and swore vengeance upon the whole Roseman clan. He must have really been spitting venom because Lou took him seriously.

For over two weeks, Big Lou and a few of his buddies would camp out on the roof of his house. With rifles cocked and Nannie's hot coffee to keep them warm and alert throughout the night, their eyes adjusted to the darkness as they scanned the dirt road leading up to the house. The tiniest noise from the surrounding woods would cause them to pop up at attention and release the safety on their guns. A tree branch breaking, the wind, the old house settling...any sound served as a release for the adrenalin that allowed Big Lou to stay on guard and protect his girls.

Night after night this went on and on. With each breaking of the dawn, a weary Lou would thank his fellow watchmen and retire to bed for a few hours sleep. The end of the story is anticlimactic. The hobo never came calling. There is no legendary tale of the Shootout of Newburg being passed down from generation to generation. There is only the story of a man who loved his family and who would go to any length to protect them. As sweet and noble as that sounds, I'd like to point out that if he wouldn't have had rail rats to dinner then he never would've had to sleep on his roof. But then again, I can be a bit critical at times.

Nana was bright and beautiful in every way. I'm sure she had her faults. Who doesn't? I certainly never saw them. She was funny, always smiling, loved by all and, in her own way, tough like her father.

On September 15, 1940, Nana married Harold Kruse, my Papa. He was a wonderful man, a great husband, a proud soldier on the WWII medical ships, and a super dad to my mom who was born six years later.

Papa told me once that Nana was very self conscious about the fact that she had lost the tip of her thumb after getting it caught in a sewing machine. I saw that thumb a thousand times and it never seemed like a big deal to me but I guess it was to her. She was also diabetic. I've recently become more aware of what it means to be diabetic as the result of a brief relationship with a woman who was Type 1. I watched her administer her shots throughout the day and was with her when she'd wake up in the middle of the night from low blood sugar. As an adult and knowing what I now know, it breaks my heart to think that Nana ever had to go through that. I hate that she was ever scared or that she experienced any discomfort. I wish she would have had exposure to the medical care that is available today. That a doctor could tell her the disease is more manageable than she realizes. I've done a couple of performances to raise money for Juvenile Diabetes Research Foundation (http://www.jdrf.org) and hope one day they will find a cure.

Everyone has someone they love the way I loved Nana and they don't deserve to suffer...ever...from Diabetes or any other disease. Another reason why I know there isn't an omniscient, omnipotent, omnipresent god. If indeed that source of love and light existed, he/she/it would never have let my Nana suffer for a single minute. Call me selfish, but that is all the proof I need that we are on our own and our greatest responsibility is to take care of each other.

In addition to being a diabetic, Nana had back problems. Not "Oh my back is sore. I think I need a heating pad" types of problems. More the "slipped disc causing numbness and pain to shoot down my legs" types of problems. I only knew of these issues because I would hear other adults ask how she was feeling or because my mother told me years later. Being in Nana's presence gave me no indication that she was anything less than happier than a puppy with two peckers. If you've ever met a puppy in that condition then you know that is one happy puppy. Nana's face would light up the moment she opened the door and saw me and Jarrod standing on her porch. It was always a hug and a "Hi T. Hi J-Bird." Goddamn...she loved us and we knew it.

We loved playing wiffle ball together. I still enjoy playing it with my own kids. Growing up, Nana was always the pitcher. Jarrod and I took turns batting. Home plate was a beat up yellow frisbee, first and third were fence posts, and second base was an old tree stump. Regardless of what kind of pain Nana may have been in, she never turned us down when we asked her to go out and play with us. We'd stay out in her little backyard for hours. I have no idea what my parents and Papa did inside while we were out rounding the bases, but Nana just pitched and pitched and pitched. She gave us her all.

Nana and Papa had no problem spoiling my brother and me. As a single dad I try not to take my kids out and buy them something every time we're together. I don't always succeed, but I do try. It probably isn't the best thing to do but it sure is hard to avoid. We should be focusing on just being together but it's so much fun to see the look on their faces when they go into their bedroom and there's a new pony book or the hot, new hockey stick.

Sometimes Nana would just go down to the little drugstore on the corner, or as she called it, the confectionery, and pick something up for us. I've never heard anyone else use that word. I Googled it to see what it meant and it's a store that mainly deals in sweets and things for the serious baker. I'm sure this place had its share of flour and eggs but it also carried everything else from baseball cards to tablets of drawing paper. She'd call our goodies "surprises" and we loved whatever she'd have for us.

Once in a while she and Papa would get fancy and put the surprise at the end of a long piece of yarn that started at the front door and made its way all throughout the house. It would weave through the kitchen, the bedrooms, closets, and usually end up in the bathtub or in a drawer. The yarn on my surprise was always blue and Jarrod's was green to match the color of the carpets in our bedrooms. We learned early on that you had to find your surprise pretty quickly because if the other guy found his first the thrill was shot. Nana and Papa always got us the exact same thing. No preference was ever shown. We were their only grandkids, my mom is an only child, and they made us feel like we were the only kids on the entire planet.

Nana worked at Missouri Baptist College for many years. Originally she worked in the snack bar and would chat with the students in between their classes. All the kids called her "Ma" and she became so popular that there would often be a line at the cash register because everyone would stop and talk to her as she took their money for the food. Where our bookmobile librarian held us up with her chit chat,

Nana would have to remind kids to be on their way. She was so good for morale that eventually she got offered a position in Student Affairs. I don't exactly know what that position was but there's a good chance it was created just for her. She had a desk in the student lounge with a fish bowl on it. The fish bowl had water in it but no fish-only a sign that read *'Invisible Piranha.'* I never did stick my hand in that bowl.

The job at MoBap was perfect for Nana. She was a people person and could light up any room she walked into. I remember when the faculty roasted her. A roast is where an individual is given a banquet in their honor. Friends, family, and co-workers take turns telling stories and taking jabs at the roastee in a showing of love. One needs to be pretty thick skinned to be the subject of a good roast and Nana loved every minute of it. I sat right up front and recorded the entire evening for her on my little tape recorder. Obviously, all of the material was as clean as a whistle because it was a baptist school. I was actually hearing racier material in my first grade classroom, but it wasn't meant for Comedy Central. It was meant for Nana and she was in her element. Many years earlier she was in charge of organizing banquets at her church and I have seen the photos. Her elaborate costumes, well orchestrated skits, perfect comedic timing, and love of being on stage made those banquets unforgettable to everyone in attendance.

When I was in my late teens and early twenties I used to stop by and visit my grandparents once a week or so. I lived not far away and it was fun to just pop in and see them.

In 1989, I was dating a young lady that I met while spinning records at a small, neighborhood bar called Geno's in south St. Louis. I can't remember the girl's name, we didn't see each other very long, but she was adorable. Like a younger, thinner Sally Struthers. Anyway, I've always had a passion for rescuing animals which is why I'm involved with Best Friends Animal Society today. My conversations with Bob Barker have certainly deepened my desire to make a difference in the pet population, but I've always believed that animals that need rescuing from a pound or shelter should be the first look for anyone who wants to add a pet to the family.

I had just rented a disgustingly large apartment on Chippewa Street and thought a dog would make the place feel more like a home. "Young Sally" and I went down to the shelter and immediately fell in love with a yellow lab that was about 2 years old. The first thing I did was take him over to meet Nana. I knew as a young girl she had raised a baby alligator in her bathtub and later given it to the St. Louis Zoo, but I don't believe she had ever had a dog. I decided to drop by and introduce her to my new best friend.

As the playful pup licked all over her face, Nana convinced me that this dog was going to be too big to keep in an apartment and would be much happier in a home with a yard. She had a gift for making her point without overstating. "Young Sally", who still lived with her parents, and I fizzled out shortly thereafter and she ended up keeping Archie (named after the character in *All In The Family*). I guess I believed in nice parting gifts even back then.

Nana's health began to deteriorate in the fall of 1993. Papa checked her into the hospital and I went to visit her everyday. By this time I was Rick Idol on the radio at night and working on my show material during the day. I had plenty of things happening to stay busy but I couldn't keep my mind off of Nana's condition. Somehow you just know when someone is not going to get better. I'm not psychic (no one is-regardless of what the neon sign in the storefront window says) but I felt that each visit I made to her hospital room could very well be the last time I'd see her.

My girlfriend at the time, Debbie, knew how much I was hurting and did everything she could to lend support and comfort. I've always found performing to be the best form of therapy. The only time I've ever been truly able to escape what is bothering me is when I'm on stage or playing with my kids.

One night while I was on the air, I mentioned to the tens of thousands of listeners that my grandmother was sick. I told of how she had worked at MoBap a while back and how the students called her "Ma." Saying it out loud somehow made me feel a little better. Instantly the request lines started ringing off the hook. I thought it was just people calling up with well wishes or words of comfort, but I could hear my intern saying things like "That sounds like her," and "I will certainly tell him. He'd love to hear that." People who knew Nana were calling in to share stories about her and how she had touched their lives. It was an incredible outpouring of love.

I saw my Nana for the last time in late October of '93. When I went to her hospital room, she was pretty drugged up and out of it but could still manage to say "Hi T" when I walked in. She definitely knew I was there with her. I recently contributed to my friend Matthew Cossolotto's book, *The Power Of A Promise,* and told him of my final words to her. I bent down, kissed her forehead and said "I promise to always make you proud of me." She smiled. I will always remember how soft her skin was. The next day she was gone.

I am not a fan of funerals. I don't think it does anyone a bit of good to sit around a gloomy funeral parlor and shed tears of sadness. It seems borderline disrespectful to the deceased to put the body on display and have their loved ones parade by and gawk at them laying motionless in a casket covered in clown makeup and wearing an outfit they only wore once while they were alive. They're not seeing who the person really was and it taints the memory. I've chosen to be cremated. It's in my Last Will and Testament. The ashes are to be divided up between my kids and they can do with them as they please. It's the memory and the love that matter. Not my crumbs in an overpriced urn.

Nana's funeral, however, was different. It was more of a celebration. In attendance were past students from the college, friends from church, and neighbors. It was packed. Oddly enough there were more people laughing than crying. Everyone was there to share what this remarkable woman had meant to them and how she had touched their lives. Mom and Papa asked me to speak. I don't remember a single word I said because I didn't prepare anything in advance. I spoke from my heart as I looked out over a sea of smiling faces and heads nodding in agreement with my words of praise. After the burial, my mom and I took Papa to lunch. He was silent. His soulmate had been taken away. The loss of Nana was beyond painful for me but it must have been devastating to Papa.

I feel Nana with me always and every now and again I will see a trace of her. Her picture sits on my bookshelf, her name is tattooed on my arm next to the names of my children, and I smile when I see Kiki chewing in the same manner Nana used to. The night before I recorded my first motivational speaking DVD, *The Choice Is Yours,* back in St. Louis in March of 2009, I drove by Nana and Papa's old house and parked my rental car in the street out front.

As I sat there reminiscing, an irresistible urge to knock on the door came over me. A young woman answered. I introduced myself and told her why I was interrupting her quiet evening at home. She must have read it in my eyes, or maybe she just wanted to get me inside. Either way, she welcomed me in. I walked through the entire house with her and spoke of the memories that were quickly rushing back. I looked out the back window of the kitchen and saw our old wiffle ball field. The woman had only lived there a few months but I told her that her new home was filled with old love and laughter. If her walls could talk there'd be nothing but goodness.

Upon leaving, I thanked her for her hospitality and invited her to my taping the next day. I hope she showed up. I didn't get her name but I'll be sending a copy of this book to her mailbox. I hope she reads it and knows how grateful I am for allowing me to relive such happy times.

Like it or not, we are influenced by those with whom we surround ourselves. The great business philosopher Jim Rohn often said, "You are the sum of the five people closest to you." If that is the case then I'm currently doing pretty well. In order to be successful in any area of life you must associate with those who lift you higher, who are strong where you are weak, and who share your vision. It's the reason I tell my kids to stay away from the troublemaker on the school bus and also the reason I spend so much time in my hotel room on the road preferring writing and reading to boozing and partying. It's much more than an issue of how others perceive you, it's an issue of integrity-of how you perceive yourself.

One of my favorite sayings is *"A clear conscious is the softest pillow"* and I'm here to tell you that I sleep like a baby with a belly full of breast milk every night. I'm proud of who I am and that is because I have always kept company with people who are proud of who they are.

In 2010, my ex-wife and I relocated both of our households to New England to provide a better life for the kids. We wanted better schools and a better environment for them to be raised in. We chose a community with a sense of neighborhood pride. We wanted our children to grow up where people did things for one another without asking "What's in it for me?"

Long before becoming a father, I realized just how fortunate I was to have had the types of people in my life that I did. Though not all of these individuals would have the staying power of Nana's influence, they all contributed in positive ways. I had also encountered people, both personally and professionally, who attempted to hold be back, diminish my dreams, or stifle my passion. They were unsuccessful, as most naysayers turn out to be, but they were present nonetheless.

Eventually, I created a technique that minimized the amount of negative influences in my life, thus maximizing the positives.

In the summer of 2009, I introduced the TN Tier System as a way to help my coaching clients who were experiencing difficulty with organization and time management. The TNTS consisted of four levels of association and personal interaction, focusing on the awareness of the roles different people play in your personal or professional life.

For the sake of giving a clear example, I'll use my own personal Tiers to demonstrate the concept and you can then, if you so choose, incorporate your associations to create your own.

For me, Tier 4 includes the people I meet in airports who are kind enough to come up and say "Caught your show and loved it," or "Don't I know you from somewhere?" These interactions are short and sweet and usually involve nothing more than a handshake, a toothy smile, and a "Thank You" on my part. I'm always flattered and happy to take a moment with them. I'm well aware that I will most likely never see this person again but that exchange will stay with them long after it is over and could possibly result in them supporting/watching my future projects. Even if you are just two ships passing in the night make sure your deck is clean...you never know.

Tier 3 consists of those with whom I am working with on a corporate event or seminar. We'll be together for a couple of weeks and need to establish a mutually beneficial relationship. There may be some disagreements or differences of opinion but it is in both of our best interests to overcome them and work toward a common solution. Whether or not we ever share the same craft services table again in the future is not important. Completing the task at hand is the goal and I always prefer to maintain a decorum that allows both parties to walk away with a minty fresh taste in the mouth.

Tier 3's are people that pop in and out of our lives without warning. My friend Jenna is my favorite Tier 3. Jen is beautiful, smart, and talented. I remember the first time I saw her. Her band was playing at the Viper Room in Hollywood. I stopped in with some friends because I was planning my birthday party there. She absolutely blew me away. She was on stage singing the most beautiful song I'd ever heard. The lyrics spoke of "moving like water" which is exactly what she was doing in her tight, blue suede pants. She is rockstar meets poet and I was hooked. I made my way over to her after she finished her set and it was love or somethin' like it from the get go. That was a long time ago and when we see each other now it's as if we never said goodbye. I feel comfortable sharing my most personal secrets with her. There is such strong chemistry between us that someone passing us on the street would assume we were on our honeymoon. We love each other on our own cosmic level but not in a way that makes it impossible for us to be apart and live our own lives. Going a year or two with no contact is not unusual for us, but we both know we're there for one another and always will be.

Tier 2 is when things start getting closer to home and when you need to start paying closer attention. Though Jenna is certainly welcome at Casa de Newton anytime, I generally distinguish a Tier 3 from a Tier 2 by asking myself if I'd invite this person to my home. I don't throw a lot of parties and like to keep the homestead rather low key, but I'd let a Tier 2 in for a plate of nachos. These are people you've known for a long time and have a clear concept of who they truly are as individuals. There is a level of trust and respect. A good example of a Tier 2 is my friend and executive producer of *The Price Is Right Live!* stage show, Andy Felsher.

I first met Andy nearly ten years ago when Fremantle Media launched a stage version of *The Price Is Right*. The idea was to take this traveling set out on the road so fans of the TV show who couldn't attend a taping in Hollywood could experience the excitement of their favorite pricing games in person and win some great prizes.

Andy has game shows flowing through his veins and was the perfect choice to be put at the helm of this new project. We opened the show together in Reno, NV, in 2002 and instantly took a liking to each other. Over the years, we've enjoyed countless unsweetened iced teas in more hotel restaurants in more cities than either of us can recall. We have kids the same age and always enjoy sharing tales of fatherhood. When I was auditioning to take over for Bob Barker on the television show, Andy worked closely with me in preparation and I will always be grateful to him for putting in the extra time to show me things in my performance that I wasn't seeing for myself. I'm proud to be a part of this franchise and Andy knows that he can always count on me to give it all I've got while I'm on stage. Work relationships that remain strong and also evolve into good friendships are a rare treasure. Andy is the exception to the rule and tops my Tier 2 list.

That brings us to Tier 1, and Tier 1's are just what you would imagine them to be. Your parents, your children, your significant other, your long time and trusted business partner, and *yourself*. A Tier 1 will run into a burning building to rescue your favorite teddy bear. A Tier 1 is someone you'd leave a pile of cash in front of without bothering to count it. A Tier 1 is someone who I would let use my private toilet...and that's really saying something. You depend on them and they depend on you. You communicate without speaking and can't imagine feeling a sense of wholeness without them in your life.

There is no limit to the amount of Tier 1's you could or should have in your life. The more the better. But that placement must be earned over time. Not only must others prove their worthiness in your Tier 1 arena but you must earn your place in their's.

My friend Ken Botelho is a Tier 1. Kenny has done more for me professionally and personally than anyone. I've learned many valuable life lessons from him and hold his friendship near and dear to my heart.

His family is my family and I know if anything ever happened to me that my children would always be watched over from afar. KB is Tony Soprano meets your good ol' Uncle Joe. He is trustworthy and devoted to those around him. He's one of the few people on the planet who's opinion I value and isn't shy about kicking my ass when I need him to in order to set me straight. With a Tier 1 you speak freely, laugh loudly, and love deeply.

Look around you. Unless you're reading this in bed with a bowl of ice cream resting on your belly, there are people within spitting distance of you. Who are they? What role are they playing in your life? Who have you associated with today and how did that exchange contribute to your life? If it was not a positive experience that resulted in some sort of forward motion why were you wasting your time?

Make a point to invest the time necessary to reassess your relationships and consider utilizing the TN Tier System to see what is what. It is my gift to you. Use it wisely in order to make absolutely certain that the people currently in your life are adding to who you want to be and not detracting from who you are.

No one had a more positive impact on me than my grandmother. We would go to Nana and Papa's house every Sunday afternoon. I'm sure sometimes I moaned and groaned about it. As a kid there were a million other things I would have rather been doing, but today I would pay a king's ransom for just a couple of hours in her living room. To sit on the couch with her and do a jigsaw puzzle. To take a walk. To go to White Castle with her. To introduce her to my kids. To let them experience her special kind of love. To play just one more game of wiffle ball.

CHAPTER 3
MY YELLOW BRICK ROAD

Going so soon? I wouldn't hear of it. Why, my little party
is just beginning.
-Wicked Witch of the West, *Wizard of Oz*

I DO NOT BELIEVE in miracles. It appears that many people are confused as to what the true definition of a miracle even is. I can't blame them. Even Webster's dictionary plays a little "cover my tail" by giving the following two definitions of this overused and misunderstood noun.

1) *A surprising and welcome event that is not explicable by natural or scientific laws and is considered to be divine.* And, 2) *A highly improbable or extraordinary event, development, or accomplishment.*

The first definition covers the religious aspect, such as when God saw fit to let the New York Giants beat the 18-0 Patriots in Super Bowl XLII. I'm still astounded by that one and, even now, look to the heavens to see if there's any trace of a divine being snickering at those of us here in New England.

The second definition basically says the same thing only seems to be tailored more towards us non-believers. How politically correct. Separation...the cornerstone of America.

Please don't mistake my skepticism for cynicism. I've witnessed some pretty amazing things in my day. The births of my kids, Mason and Kiki, were life changing events that brought tears of joy and made me look at the world in a new, overprotective, and loving way. But based on the definition above, the birth of a child is not a *miracle*. Science tells us how babies are made. We watch the Discovery Channel and witness the mating rituals of the animal kingdom. Research has proven, beyond any doubt, that when the man's sperm successfully fertilizes the woman's egg the process has begun. It's disappointing that science does not properly inform us of all that leads up to the actual fertilization- good oral hygiene, the search for the perfect opening line, dinner at Chili's, etc- but I suppose that is what older siblings and premium cable channels are for.

Growing up in Missouri, I recall the countless news stories of tornados causing massive destruction. Graphic video footage of a twister is incredible, powerful, and beautiful in its own way, but it is not a *miracle*. Again, science tells us that tornadoes occur when the right combination of temperature and humidity meet to form thunderclouds. They are awesome forces of nature, but easily explained. What *is* miraculous to me is that there are still people who choose to live in trailer parks knowing the patterns history has shown us...but that's none of my business.

Individuals who conquer a disease often say that their recovery was a miracle. I use the word conquer in honor of a woman named Victoria Barmak who recently posted the following message on my Facebook page after attending one of my presentations.

"I am not going to call myself a breast cancer survivor. Survivor connotes I have been a victim. NO WAY! I am a breast cancer CONQUEROR!!!!!! Thank you Todd Newton!"

There is no need to thank me. Victoria is the hero and her story shows that the human body, with the assistance of knowledgable health care professionals and decades of research, has the ability to heal. God did not choose her over other patients. Her body healed! By definition *no miracle occurred* because we can explain what took place and how.

Sunsets can be awe inspiring. Seeing dolphins play in the ocean is unforgettable. Winning the lottery when on the verge of losing your home to foreclosure would be enough to make anyone drop to their knees and give thanks. But there is no such thing as a miracle. If Elvis and Marilyn Monroe show up at my next birthday party then, and only then, can we revisit the issue. Until that happens my mind is made up.

All of this being said, I do believe that there are moments in our lives when everything changes and our life takes on a new direction. Decisive moments. Moments that really do take your breath away like only a first kiss or a baby's smile can. I've had many. The greatest of which were when I held my kids for the first time. The magic of these moments comes not from how many of them you can accumulate, but rather how much you are able to appreciate them when they happen.

In improvisational comedy (improv) we are trained to slow moments down and soak everything we can get from them before moving on to the next one. I've gotten pretty good at this over the years and, in hindsight, now realize I've had more of these life altering moments than perhaps I initially realized.

One particular day in the spring of 1989 will always stand out. I had just turned nineteen years old and was attending classes at St. Louis Community College. I fully admit that I did not take my studies very seriously. I knew that what I wanted to do with my life could not be taught in a classroom unless Wolfman Jack decided to hang up his headphones and become a college professor. I only enrolled because it's what you do after high school and it seemed to make my parents happy. Plus, there wasn't anything else happening in my life that prevented college from being my main focal point...until one day.

Every city in America has them. That one rag (weekly newspaper) that is filled with ads telling you what band is playing where, who has the best beer specials, and page after page of massage parlors. In L.A. it's called *LA Weekly*. New York has the *Village Voice*. St. Louis has the *Riverfront Times*.

The *RFT*'s website states that it has a circulation of 100,000 but, due to the pass along factor, the paper reaches nearly a quarter of a million people each week. It's available just about everywhere people who drink hard music and listen to loud liquor are sold. It offers the occasional insightful article, but every college kid grabbed one because the price was right. Free.

One afternoon, while thumbing through the classifieds, I stumbled upon the most basic yet eye catching add my young baby blues had ever seen. I have contacted *RFT* in hopes of attaining the exact ad to place here but have been unsuccessful due mainly to the passage of time. The original consisted of little more than the following.

MC NEEDED FOR AREA NIGHTCLUB
CALL 618-XXX-XXXX

The 618 area code means the nightclub in mention was located in Illinois. This is a key piece of information in that Illinois laws are considerably different than the laws of Missouri. I knew that establishments on the east side of the Mississippi River are allowed to stay open much later than those in the Show Me State. I was also aware, through nothing more than high school locker room chatter, that full nudity was also allowed in certain places once you crossed the bridge. What the St. Louis bar hoppers would do, and I'm assuming is probably still the practice, is hang out in "The Lou" until the usual 1am closing time, then cross the river and stay out until the sun comes up.

It couldn't hurt to call. I dialed the number in the ad and nearly fell out of my chair when the woman on the other end of the phone informed me which nightclub was in search of a Master of Ceremonies. The OZ. The role to be filled? A new "voice" for their male strip show, "The Wizards of OZ." Now, unless you are from the St. Louis area you probably will never have the full understanding of what role The OZ actually plays in the history of the town. To say that it is legendary is a gross understatement. As a matter of fact, in January of 2012, I went home to visit my parents and took a drive out to The OZ. It was around 3pm when I pulled into the old parking lot and turned off my car. I just sat there and remembered the good times. This is not *just* a nightclub. It's an institution. The OZ is to St. Louis what Studio 54 is to New York and what the Whiskey-A Go-Go is to Los Angeles. You remember your first trip to The OZ like you remember your first bicycle. Athletes and celebrities frequented the mirrored utopia and seeing yourself glowing in the black lights became a rite of passage. We danced there, fell in love there, lost and found ourselves there. Granted, The OZ's best days are probably long in the past, but in the 80's there was no place else anyone wanted to be. And I had a shot to work there.

I would love to have a photo of the outfit I wore to that job interview. All I am able to recall is pulling up to a mobile home in my maroon Cutlas Supreme and not being able to get out of the car. The trailer served as the main office for the company that owned The OZ and a few other nightclubs.

After collecting myself as best I could, I walked up the black iron stairs, knocked, and was shown inside. The door creaked as I entered and it was clear the interior of the mobile home did not match the glitz and glamour that The OZ was known for. The club was all strobe lights and disco balls whereas the trailer was halogen lamps and army green filing cabinets. The OZ was known for its arena-like sound system, but not a note of music would be heard here. Only the static and chatter of an AM talk radio station.

I shook the hand of the man who would soon become someone I greatly admired...manager of The OZ, Jim Greenwald. Jimmy had a big Rolex, a larger than life persona, and a smile that would make any top notch car dealer or politician envious. Everything about him said style and charisma and I instantly knew I wanted to spend as much time in his company as possible.

Also present was a woman named Tina who has since passed away. Tina sat behind her large desk as a cloud of menthol cigarette smoke swirled above her fire engine red hair. She was a doll and everything you'd expect in a woman in charge of multiple party palaces in East St. Louis to be. The OZ was the sexy entity but this trailer was the brains. Mission Control.

I was an absolute pile of young, midwestern nerves that day and cannot recall with any degree of accuracy what transpired. The meeting could have lasted ten minutes or two hours. I really have no idea. I can't remember what they asked me or what I told them. For this reason, and many others, I thank Jimmy Greenwald for a recent email in which he recalls our first meeting so that I may share it with you.

The "Wizards of OZ" male dance review was a popular attraction at OZ niteclub in Sauget, Illinois, every Friday night. The entertaining show for ladies only, was tastefully done yet sexy. OZ club manager Jimmy "Holliday" Greenwald began the show as the MC with upbeat positive energy. Jimmy was in his mid 30's and got the ladies charged up for the show with his off the cuff impromptu manner of announcing the dancers and keeping the atmosphere alive. The Wizards show and the nightly audience began to take a major toll on his voice.

Jimmy was diagnosed with polyp nodules on his vocal chords which were fixed with minor surgery. This was a sign it was time to give up the "MIC". He soon returned to the management of the club with one of his first duties to begin the search for a new voice of the Wizards.

ENTER TODD NEWTON

A large media blitz started, highlighted with an ad in the entertainment newspaper the River Front times which is the pulse of the nite life news in St Louis. Interviews were held at the main office at OZ. On one particular Tuesday morning, in walked a young 18 year old, soon to be a wunderkind named Todd Newton from South St Louis County. The rest is history. Todd impressed Jimmy and Tina with his looks, confidence, voice quality, and a maturity well beyond his years. Todd and Jimmy began working together, and Todd took to the job as a born natural. He mirrored Jimmy for just a short time and soon began his own dynasty as an announcer and entertainer.

Jimmy was relieved and elated at Todd's instant success, which gave the show a new lift and a huge boost! Todd's rise to stardom in the entertainment business, locally and now nationally, was no surprise to Jimmy and the crowds at the clubs in St. Louis.

He had it all. He was born to be onstage.

Little did I know that my life was about to change in so many ways. One day I'm delivering pizzas for date money and the next thing you know I'm on stage screaming into a microphone in front of hundreds of charged up women and putting some real coin in my pocket. I was paid $100 a night which is a lot of cash for a kid. I felt like Trump and immediately developed an appreciation for the feeling of having money. Like the old saying goes, *"People who say that money can't buy happiness...don't have any."*

The Wizards of Oz was a special group of guys. Male strip shows weren't as commonplace in the late eighties and early nineties as they are today. Today, you can locate a revue just about anywhere, any night of the week. The Wizards were different. These guys were local celebrities and if you wanted to see them you had to be at the OZ on Friday night. Birthday parties, bachelorette parties, divorce parties, girls night out...you name it! Women came from far and wide and made up any excuse to get away from their husbands and boyfriends to come see guys like Johnny Angel, Nature Boy, Marc Anthony, Rico, Hollywood, Steve Thunder, Miguel, Sampson, and the rest of the boys shake their money makers. And they made some money. Cash came flying out of purses so freely you'd think you were at an old time church revival. The women loved every minute of it. They were watching a real production with real performers who put everything they had into each performance They had to. Their livings depended on it.

Looking back, I truly believe that watching these guys work gave me my first real appreciation for the time I spend on stage. A performer owes it to the audience to be "on" from the moment the lights go down until we take our final bow. People pay hard earned money to come see us. For many of them the show is an escape from a stressful life or a well deserved break from monotony. It sounds cliche, but no one in the audience cares if the person on stage is having a bad day, if our throat hurts, if we're fighting with our significant other, or even if our house just burned down. *"I bought my ticket now entertain me!"* is the mentality and I respect that. That's how I feel when I'm an audience member. The Wizards felt the same way and wanted to knock it out of the park every show.

Horsing around backstage with the Wizards
before a show in Peoria, IL. 1990.

These guys put thought into their costumes, rehearsed their choreography, spent hours a day in the gym working on their bodies, and, above all, understood that the show didn't center around just one dancer. When one of us made money, we all made money. The importance of "all for one and one for all" was demonstrated to me in the dressing room one night after a show.

One of the guys, Michael St. John was his stage name, felt as if I had been working the audience up for other dancers more so than for him. It was no secret to anyone that the wilder the women became the more generous they were with their dollar bills. I would often contrive bogus credits about the guys appearing on Oprah, MTV, whatever. I'm sure no one believed any of it but the guys always liked it. Anyway, Michael's temper was enhanced by the use of steroids and he had apparently reached his boiling point. I had reached mine, as well, and finally got sick of him mouthing off. The show was over. I told him I'd beef it up next week and to just drop it. Instead he chose to drop me. This 6'4" perfectly sculpted specimen hauled off and delivered the most perfectly placed punch in the history of barroom scuffles. It hit me square in the face. A direct hit. I'm convinced it was the strongest impact the human skull can absorb without caving in. No one has ever hit another human being with more force, I'm sure of it. Immediately the rest of the guys, who had been standing back and letting us work things out ourselves, jumped in and broke it up. I threw a couple of wild punches in retaliation but didn't connect. My eyes were watering so badly I couldn't see a thing. I tasted blood and thought for sure my nose was broken, but all I really cared about were my teeth. I had just gotten my braces off a few months before.

After making sure that I had suffered no facial deformities, we shook hands. That is how you handle disagreements with people who mean something to you. No one called the cops or filed a lawsuit. Two men admitting their faults and growing closer as a result. Michael is a doctor now and still a very good friend. The incident is indicative of how tight we all were and how passionate we were about the show we were lucky enough to be a part of. It also showed the boys that I could take a monster of a punch.

There wasn't one particular star in the Wizards of Oz. We were all headliners and contributed to the show's success. It was about everyone...and that included the new MC. The kid now known as T.J. Blue.

I know it's a corny name. T.J. stems from my first and middle names in reverse order. Blue came from a lovely young woman who, on my first night at the club, told me I had pretty eyes. She was a smooth talker as were many of the ladies I had the pleasure of meeting and spending time with as a result of my new job. I knew with a position like this you had to have a flashy name. I was in show business now. I couldn't be the only guy using his real identity. On top of that, I was pretty certain that my parents weren't all that thrilled about my new affiliation with the show so I thought a stage name might protect me (and them) from anyone coming in and recognizing Jim and Anne's boy as the chatterbox screaming "C'mon ladies! What you give is how they live!"

It's pretty safe to say there aren't too many people in today's work force that cannot wait to go to work but, back then, I absolutely lived for Friday nights. I can remember with crystal clear clarity and detail the drive across the Jefferson Barracks bridge, onto Route 3, and straight into Illinois with my windows down and my favorite cassettes blaring. Music always gets me in the zone. Even today I have a special pre-show playlist on my iPhone that I only listen to before going onstage. Back then, the perfect tune just reinforced that feeling I had of being on top of the world.

Eventually, the OZ sign would begin to appear off in the distance. The unmistakable orange letters would grow bigger and brighter like the sun rising above the muddy Mississippi. Getting even closer, I would begin to see the line of cars waiting to pull into the parking lot. I'm going to guess the club held 500-600 women, and they showed up in droves to see the Wizards. Unless it was a holiday where the women had to be off with their families, we could pretty much count on a full house.

Our show seemed to have had the same appeal as a rock concert because bachelorettes and other groups of giddy girls would line up an hour or so in advance just to get a seat close to the stage. What they failed to take into consideration, of course, was that there really wasn't a "bad" seat in the house. Not because our stage was located in the middle of the club with seats on all four sides, but because the guys made sure they allotted plenty of time in their routines to visit every corner and every booth. No hungry woman went unfed.

Being the host of this show introduced me to two very instrumental things in my life. The first was the thrill of being in the limelight. Up until that point I had never had people stand up and cheer when I was introduced and that is a feeling I wish everyone could experience at least once. Love it or hate it, there is no thrill quite like it. Jimmy would bring the lights down and do the initial welcome. My intro music would then kick on. I'd walk onstage to the sound of pulsating rock music music while smoke machines and strobe lights brought everyone in attendance to complete sensory overload. It was Jim who made a big deal out of me and, in turn, made the audience treat me like a big deal. He could have just as easily handed me the microphone with no intro whatsoever and I would have amounted to little more than a narrative voice shuffling one dancer onto the stage after another. But instead, he gave me an identity and built me up like a superstar. He was the epitome of professional generosity and the reason I try to be equally as generous to my co-hosts and colleagues today.

Being known as "The Man Behind The Mic" and "The Voice Of Choice" also had other perks. Though not yet old enough to drink, I was suddenly welcomed with open arms into any other nightclub in the area. I never had to wait in line, rarely paid a tab, and wasn't introduced to a cover charge until several years later. To this day, even though I'm not a club person, I still refuse to even consider going anywhere where a customer is expected to pay just for the privilege of walking through the front door. If there is an admission price there better be a show. I better be entertained. The fact that it has become the standard for people to A) wait in line, B) pay a cover, and C) pay even *more* to drink is absolutely absurd to me. I respect a person's right to make money and run a business but some things are just out of my comprehension.

It didn't take a genius to see that the new job was going to lead to the demise of my relationship with my high school sweetheart. Kelly was such a doll and everything an average teenager could ask for. But my life had suddenly become anything *but* average. Knowing that her boyfriend was spending every weekend surrounded by beautiful women became too much for her and we eventually parted ways. She went off to college and I went off to work.

After four years of being almost inseparable, Kelly's absence left a big whole in my heart. Just when I needed a pick-me-up to get me out of my funk, Jimmy asked if I would be interested in adding the duty of hosting the Thursday night sexy legs contest to my OZ belt. More money, more exposure...and more women. Sweet Kelly quickly became a sweet memory.

If the Friday night male dance review was considered crowded then the Thursday night atmosphere can only be described as electric. Good looking men and women drowning themselves in unlimited well drinks and draft beer for the price of a ten dollar bill. It wasn't unheard of to reach maximum capacity within two hours of opening the doors. Those folks who had to be at work on Friday morning just accepted the fact that they were going to be running on half a tank when they got to the office because *everyone* came to The OZ on Thursdays and *everyone* stayed until the lights came on at 4am.

In all honesty, the sexy legs contest had very little to do with a woman's legs. This is a shame because the shape and contour of finely toned and tanned drumstick is one of nature's masterpieces. I'm a leg guy and a very appreciative one, at that. The contest, however, awarded $100 cash to the woman who could best incite the crowd into a near frenzy and there were no rules. The girls, most of them quite stunning, would dance and shimmy their way around the stage like the pros that many of them were. Articles of clothing were shed, men from the audience would be pulled out and used as props, and the crowd would eat it up. The noise level would get so loud that my microphone became virtually useless. The contest would take on a life of its own.

My only real duty was to introduce each contestant and then leave them out there for as long as she could hold the interest of the inebriated patrons. For those of you who are reading this and remembering the Thursdays we shared together, I'm sure you are wondering if I am going to mention one woman in particular...The Bohemian Potato Farmer. I'm quite certain she was not Bohemian, nor had she ever farmed potatoes, but she became an OZ legend and deservedly so.

The Bohemian, who's real name I never learned, was not a feather's weight shy of 300 pounds. She was a big, big girl. Every good host knows how to build anticipation and I would always save The Farmer (credit Jimmy Holiday for the greatest nickname of all time) for last. After all of the strippers, calendar girls, and other hopefuls had lifted their miniskirts and dropped their dignity, I would scream, "Are you ready for one more?" The audience knew what was coming and would go ballistic! Her music would blast through the speakers and out to the middle of the dance floor she would go. Sauntering, strutting, and shaking a caboose that could have been divided into three, she gave that crowd what it came for. They loved her and she never had to remove a stitch of clothing. It's safe to say that the infamous Bohemian Potato Farmer won ninety five percent of the contests she entered and she was worth every penny we paid her.

There was only woman who ever bumped the Farmer out of the running. She was a beautiful young lady named Tina who looked just like Heather Locklear and made more than her fair share of jaws drop... including mine.

Tina was straight off the pages of a magazine. Blonde, tan, and incredibly sexy. As much as I would try to talk to her she would always play the shy girl card. I'd see her and her friends walk in (I normally hung out by the door pretending to be talking to the security guys but would actually be scouting out the girls) and give her a casual smile. She'd always smile back. Never snobby or pretentious but never really giving me anything to go on either.

Tina was the exception to the rule in that she could win a sexy legs contest just for having sexy legs. Other than entering a contest at one in the morning and hiking her mini skirt up a bit, there really wasn't anything slutty about her. I became infatuated with Tina and eventually got tired of being one of the many that just admired her from afar.

After every contest, I'd take it upon myself to escort the winner back to Jimmy's office so she could collect her prize money. I used the short walk to feel out whether or not I had a chance with this girl. If I felt as if I did, I would wait around while she got paid. My lingering presence signaled to all of the bartenders, barbacks, and bouncers that I had an interest and was going to make a play. They would all respectfully back down off of their predatory haunches and pursue someone else, usually the girl who had come in second or third place that night. If I left immediately upon introducing her to Jimmy, then it was known that she was fair game.

One night, after yet another win, I took Tina's hand, walked her to the back, and didn't leave. Jimmy, sensing what was going on, left us alone in the office where we stayed and talked until closing time.

We hung out at the club together over the next couple of weeks and then I decided we needed some private time. I was still living with my parents so it was difficult to find a place where we could be alone. Most of the other women I'd met were older and had their own places, but Tina and I were the exact same age and in the same boat. Her presence on the St. Louis club scene was thanks to a poorly constructed fake Iowa driver's license produced in some guy's living room for $40. It wasn't pretty, but she certainly was and that was all it took to gain entry to any club she wished.

I put the word out that I needed a crash pad and soon one of the male dancers invited us over to his new apartment. Tina had a friend, also a beautiful blonde, so we made it a nice, little stay at home double date. We ordered some food, shot the bull, watched a movie, and then split up into separate bedrooms. I won't go into the intimate details because there aren't that many to tell.

As we made ourselves more comfortable, the stench of body odor became more and more prominent in the room. Initially I thought perhaps I was to blame, or that my buddy had left some dirty clothes laying around, but it became clear that it was coming from Tina. She smelled as if she'd just run a marathon in a snowsuit. I tried my best to focus on how beautiful she was and fight through the stench but it was no use. I had no idea how to handle the situation and felt panic coming on.

In a last ditch effort to salvage the evening, I thought perhaps there might be some cologne in the bathroom that I could "accidentally" spill into her armpits. I got up and flipped on the light but could only find a bottle of Scope mouthwash. Seeing no other option, I poured it generously over my hands and returned to where Tina was growing more and more impatient. I immediately began rubbing my hands all over her arms until she finally began gagging from a minty overdose. She said the smell of peppermint repulsed her. Can you believe that? *She* was repulsed. That was it. The mood was shot. After all of the pursuing I had done, the moment had finally arrived for us to be together and now I was forced to pull a hasty retreat.

Though certainly not like I had hoped, luck turned out to be on my side. Just as I was about to tell her that I was too tired or suggest she take a lengthy shower, there was a knock on the bedroom door. I opened it to find Tina's friend fully clothed with purse in hand. The look on her face told me things had not gone well for my buddy either.

"Tina, let's get out of here," she said.

Women will always stick together. It is an unwritten, yet well established rule. Whether it's a quick trip to the restroom or the friend who wants to go home because no one is paying attention to her, rarely do they leave one of their own behind. Tina was well aware of the sisterhood code and didn't ask any questions.

After they had left, I noticed my friend was looking a bit pale. Confidence was never in short supply with him and I couldn't imagine what possibly could have transpired that threw him for such a loop. His description of what had gone down made me queasy, and I wasn't even in the same room. In an unusually shaky voice, he explained that they were enjoying each other's company when, in the heat of passion, the girl leaned over and blew out the scented candle that was burning next to the bed. She then proceeded to try and stick it where the sun don't shine. Talk about a mood killer.. If Tina's not so fresh scent wasn't enough of a deal breaker, that candle certainly sealed the evening's fate.

I loved meeting these women. They came from all over the bi-state area and each week brought new and exciting prospects. Completely different from what I had been used to up until that point, I was now coming into contact with teachers, lawyers, businesswomen, police officers, you name it. Some of them were really interesting ladies that I got to know quite well.

The OZ doors opened to the male clientele at 11pm which meant our show needed to be over by that time. It also meant that if I could move the show along at a fairly quick pace we would finish early and have hundreds of women all to ourselves before the wolves could enter the forest. This is quite often what occurred. If I, or one of the guys, saw a young lady we were particularly interested in we'd simply let each other know. We were all very respectful of each other and never pursued someone one of our friends was looking to meet. Speeding the show along, cutting out some of my chatter, meant an easy twenty minutes of just us and them. It was bonus time and was usually all it took.

One evening I noticed a woman who had taken a bit of a shine to me. I had seen her at the show several times before. She was hard to miss. With looks that could make a preacher cuss, she was not the type of girl you typically run into at midnight in East St. Louis. She caught my attention early on and waved me over with a perfectly manicured finger. I obeyed like a hungry puppy. She had come to the club alone that night specifically to meet and hang out with me. Come to think of it, I had never seen her with anyone else. She was always alone, drinking her drink as she swayed to the music. Her name was Samantha and she spoke very slowly and seductively in a raspy, Demi Moore-like voice. I asked her to wait while I changed clothes and we could spend some time getting to know each other. She agreed.

Back in the dressing room, some of the guys were having quite a laugh at my expense and refused to fill me in on the joke at first. Eventually my pal Rico let me know that the young lady I had been talking to had been nicknamed Casper. I just assumed it was because of her blonde hair and fair complexion. It didn't matter. All I wanted to do was put on my street clothes and get back out to her. I didn't really pay much attention to it. It wasn't unheard of for a one of the guys to wind up with a girl another had dated. It's a small world, after all.

Sam and I made our way to one of the booths in the back corner of the club where the neon shadows illuminated her face. My friend Big Rob, also our head of security, took post to keep people from invading our space. I guess you could say it was the VIP section before nightclubs became pretentious enough to start labeling particular areas as such.

When the club started letting men in it was as if Sam had raw meat tied around her neck. Every man in the joint just wanted to look at her and I couldn't blame them in the least. It was similar to when a celebrity is having dinner in a restaurant and everyone takes the long way to the restroom just to get a peek. She seemed oblivious to all the attention and that attracted me to her even more. Obviously she had been a standout beauty her whole life but her focus remained solely on me and our conversation.

I liked her but I didn't like the crowd that was gathering, so I suggested we go grab a late dinner at the diner down the road. She nodded in agreement, took my hand, and we made our way out to the parking lot.

Sam's car was considerably nicer than mine so I didn't protest when she offered to drive. I opened her door for her and can remember how beautiful her legs looked as she slid into the driver's seat. She leaned over and opened my door for me, as well. It wasn't necessary, but everything she did seemed like a perfect, well orchestrated move. As I buckled my seatbelt she leaned over and gave me a soft kiss on the lips followed by a little peck on the tip of my nose. Her lips were perfect and her hair smelled of expensive shampoo.

A strange thing happened on the drive to the restaurant. Neither one of us said anything during the ten minute ride. This didn't strike me as unusual, though. The club was so loud inside that quite often your ears would still be ringing long after you've pulled out of the parking lot. Nothing seemed too terribly out of the ordinary until Sam began singing at the top of her lungs. I didn't recognize the song and the radio wasn't even on. The melody was originating in her head and the words made absolutely no sense. She was yelling about ravens and sorrow.

It was if I wasn't even in the car. She was in her own world and, to be honest, I became a little uncomfortable when the singing turned into shrieking. I looked at her as if she was going to stop at any moment and begin laughing. She didn't.

Finally, we arrived at the diner and things returned to her version of normal. I was still trying to figure it all out when we walked into the restaurant. The door had a bell on it that jingled as we entered and the waitress pointed us to a booth in the corner. Other than a trucker and another couple, we had the whole place to ourselves.

The waitress came over and took our order. I had my back to everyone else which was exactly how I wanted it. Now I could face Sam and give her my undivided attention. She, however, was scanning the place like an Army sniper. At first I thought she might be on drugs. That's a big no-no for me. I do not spend time with women who shoot, snort, smoke, or drink too much, but something told me that wasn't the case. She forced herself to return to our conversation as often as she could, but there was definitely some internal struggle happening and my patience was beginning to reach it's limit. Finally I asked her if everything was okay.

"I can't believe they followed me here," she said.

I looked around. "Who?"

Then she laid it on me. Now, I've met my share of crazies over the years but I was too young and too inexperienced to have been prepared for what was coming next. Sam, this beautiful woman that I felt so fortunate to be sharing a $4 stack of delicious diner pancakes with...saw dead people.

"Wherever I go, a band of spirits comes with me. They're not after you, it's me," as if this would somehow put my mind at ease. She went on, "They just show up and watch me."

She began pointing out where they were supposedly sitting. There was a Native American, two little girls, and a man who resembled her father. All they did was stare at her, she said, and I could see that she was growing increasingly uncomfortable.

"Why don't we just take off?" I suggested, but she didn't hear me. She was looking off into an empty corner of the diner and then she suddenly jumped out of the booth, spilling both of our drinks.

"Why won't you just leave me alone? I'm not ready to come with you. Leave...me...ALONE!!!"

And with that, she was gone. She ran out of the restaurant and jumped in her car as if someone was chasing her. Her tires shot pieces of gravel into the side of the building as she peeled out of the parking lot. I was still sitting in the booth when I saw the last of her brake lights recede into the darkness. By now the other customers, the waitress, and the cook were all staring at me. If this had been a movie, I would have delivered a witty line, thrown some cash down on the table, and walked out. But this was reality, and the reality was a crazy woman had just ran out of a diner after supposedly seeing ghosts. I, for one, did not see any ghosts and felt it was only right and perfectly acceptable under the circumstances to continue enjoying my pancakes.

As I sat there pouring syrup and replaying the last fifteen minutes over and over in my head, I remembered that she had been my ride. The waitress came over as I was finishing the last bite.

"Everything okay?" she asked.

I wasn't sure if she was referring to Sam's rant or the pancakes, but either way my answer was yes. Everything was fine. When the cab I had called from a pay phone finally arrived, I laughed to myself in the backseat as the joke from earlier that evening finally hit me. *Casper.*

The OZ Nightclub not only changed my life, it enhanced it. As I write this book I cannot imagine my journey being nearly as exciting as it has been up to this point without the OZ experience. I never graduated from college, never felt that a classroom would give me what I needed to excel, but my time at that club with those people loaded me up with valuable street knowledge. I also developed strong and lasting friendships. Johnny Angel is now a talented tattoo artist and the man who inked *"Know Thyself"* on my chest. Another former dancer is one of my attorneys. Yet another is a commercial pilot for a major airline and I always get a kick out of seeing him on one of my flights. All of them are amazing guys. True brothers.

The OZ also gave me the opportunity to develop my stage persona. The way I am on any stage is little more than a slightly exaggerated version of who I am off stage, but it's a constant evolution. As I write this chapter, I am in Ft. Lauderdale, FL, hosting *The Price Is Right Live!*. Last night was opening night at the Seminole Coconut Creek Casino and we played to an audience of over 850 people. It has been over twenty years, but I still use some of the lines I used back then to work up the OZ crowd. You know what? Those lines still work. Because of my time at OZ I know how to utilize every inch of a stage, no matter how big or small it is, and how to make every person in the audience feel as if they are in the front row. You can't learn that in a textbook. I should know, I've read hundreds of them.

And, believe it or not, in spite of all the crazy, backstage, rock n roll-type stories with various women over the years, my time at The OZ instilled within me a deep respect for the female species. Every woman I was involved with during that period was older than I was so I grew up quickly in that regard. I was nineteen learning the lessons of a twenty five year old. I learned that women want to be appreciated, adored, and understood. They want a man who pays attention and is willing to share. I also learned that when you see a woman for who she really is her beauty is multiplied many times over. As the father of a little girl, this really hits home as I want every man to see every woman for who she truly is.

I enjoy hearing from ladies that I met during that time of my life. I don't always remember the names, but the moments, the laughs, and the conversations we shared are forever etched into my mind. To all the girls that I met at The OZ, thank you for the role you played in my life... and I hope you'll forgive me if I didn't call the next day.

I dedicate this chapter to the memory of Big Rob Adams, the gentle giant. You are missed.

Chapter 4
All the Motivation I Need

*I will act now. I will walk where failures fear to walk. I will work
when failures seek rest. I will act now for now is all I have. Tomorrow
is the day reserved for the labor of the lazy. I am not lazy. Tomorrow
is the day when the failure will succeed. I am not a failure.
I will act now. Success will not wait.*
- Og Mandino

YOU PROBABLY HAVEN'T MET too many people who need to set an
alarm for 3am. If you have, then chances are none of them consistently
wake up five minutes before that alarm goes off. That happens to me
all the time.

Though I don't require a pre-dawn wake up call every morning,
it happens with enough regularity, this morning in fact, that I choose
to use it as the lead-in to a chapter that focuses on the borderline
obsessive, workaholic perfectionist I've just recently come to terms
with being.

My presentation, *The Choice Is Yours*, continues to be quite popular
at colleges and conventions due to the fact that it relates to any audience
anywhere in the world. I believe the choices we make in everyday life,
no matter how big or small, lead to the type of lives we have. We are
faced with more choices than we are even aware of. What time to wake
up. How many packs of sweetener to put in our coffee. How to handle
a confrontation. Which route to take to work. What clothes to wear.
Whether or not to join an online dating service. How long to stay on
the treadmill...it goes on and on.

I always knew I would be a disc jockey. That was never a question.
What I wanted was to become an *unforgettable* disc jockey. As a result,
I never studied or pursued anything else. I attended college, was even
inducted into my school's Walk of Fame, but never graduated. I never
felt that having a degree would make me a better entertainer and not
once has a casting agent or producer asked me about my education.
When I was sixteen years old and lugging record crates in and out of
wedding receptions and smokey taverns, I believed deep down that,
with each playing of *You Dropped A Bomb On Me*, I was one step
closer to being a star on the airwaves. Whatever the cost, I was happy
to rip open my velcro wallet and pay my dues.

This morning I woke up just before 3am to the smell of my new, twenty five dollar coffee maker brewing up some sweet Huckleberry java to start the day. By 3:15am I was on the exercise bike getting the blood flowing for the day ahead. By 5:30am I was having another cup of coffee and an egg white sandwich at Boston Logan Airport waiting for my 7:04am flight to Los Angeles and praying to a god that I don't believe exists that I'd get upgraded to first class. I didn't. I ended up sitting in that awkward seat right next to the loading door. You know the one. The seat that they tell you has extra leg room (I'm 6'3" and always appreciative of extra legroom) but actually has less because the inside of the door protrudes out about a foot and jams into your leg. Except for a brief, yet cordial, disagreement with the flight attendant strapped into the seat in front of me about whether or not it was physically possible for my laptop to shoot out from under my seat and elevate high enough into the air to blast her in the face, I slept through most of the flight. By 10:30am PST I was standing in line to pick up my rental car. At 11:15am I was northbound on the 405 freeway on my way to Burbank for a voiceover session. The new season of *Family Game Night* is on the air and doing very well.

Sometimes during the editing process a few moments that aren't critical to the outcome of the game need to be cut out. When these moments include a rule description or a fun reaction I'll come in, watch the video, and voice track the line so it can be placed back into the final cut. I always cringe a bit when I watch the show at home and hear a segment that has been placed in later, but that's just me being my own worst critic. Ultimately, it always appears seamless because we have an editing team that actually *did* go to school to learn their trade and there is no one better.

It's always great to see some of the production team. I usually hang around for a few minutes to shoot the bull but am soon reminded that I must jump back into the smallest vehicle known to man and drive to my manager's office where I will be teaching a workshop on game show hosting later that evening.

Let me tell you about my manager. Marki Costello is the queen of hosting and the queen of managers for one reason and one reason only...she is the best. Period. I once walked into her office and Marki is working the phone while horizontal on a conference room table

On the set of Family Game Night. 2011.

getting her eyebrows plucked. She's brilliant and never misses a beat. That is pure Hollywood. She is one of the few people in this world, and certainly in show business, who's opinion I trust enough to follow blindly into almost any agreement or situation. She cares for me and protects me. Every one of her clients would say the same thing. I love and respect her.

Marki and I conduct these workshops three times a year and gear them specifically toward students who are interested in learning the intricacies of hosting in our genre. After receiving my first Daytime Emmy nomination in 2011, I've noticed that people look at me as if I now know what I am talking about when it comes to hosting. It's flattering and insulting at the same time because it makes me feel as if before the nomination they just looked at me as some goofball who would host a badminton tournament at an old folk's home. The joke is on them because if paid enough I'd gladly host that tournament and the old folks would love it so much that bingo day would die out faster than Myspace.

A misconception that many people outside of showbiz have about entertainers is that the longer we're around, the more selective we become about the jobs we take. That may be true to a certain degree, but the truth is nearly everything has a price tag. When I was hosting VH1's *In Search of the Partridge Family* with Danny Bonaduce, he once told me while we were having our makeup done that he'd throw that red velvet jumpsuit back on in a minute and appear at a car dealership if the price was right. Personally, I'm a fan of appearances and the money they bring in. As long as it isn't damaging to my reputation and is a gig I know I can perform well, I'm in! I've hosted everything from belly flop contests during spring break to international beauty pageants. I'm addicted to hearing my own voice through a microphone. All I ask is that you spell my name correctly when you write the check.

These days, I love working with people who want to become hosts and who are willing to put in the time to learn how to do it properly. It sometimes upsets me when I see actors or comedians getting a prime hosting gig-not only because I want it and probably could do it ten times better-but because hosting is an art. It's *my* art. There's a science to conducting a compelling interview or presiding over a game in a way that keeps the country's attention enough to tune in again week after week. Except for the rare exception, actors aren't great hosts. Acting is really nothing more than heightened make believe and we've all been playing make believe since we were kids. As hard as it may be to understand, it is often more difficult to be yourself on camera than it is to be someone else. Don't get me wrong, I have respect for serious actors. I've been on the sets of many shows playing news anchors and the like...believe me, we're not always talking rocket surgery or brain science. You're given the words to say, a director who tells you how to say them, and a crew of professionals who's job it is to make you look as perfect as possible. Granted there are some bad actors, but there are also bad auto mechanics, bad doctors and bad burger flippers. Every profession has its cream that rises to the top and the curd that sinks to the bottom. You have to put in the work if you want to master your craft.

Smoking a cigar with Hef at the Playboy Mansion. 2000.

The people attending this particular workshop in Los Angeles were passionate about hosting. They all had their own individual ideas of what makes a host great and together we were able to carve out a vision of what a game show host should be. We did a lot of interactive discussion. I asked a couple of my friends from the game show world to stop by. We had some on camera practice, and before we knew it, the three hours had come to an end. I couldn't believe how quickly it went by and how much everyone seemed to enjoy it. As usual, I had over prepared and could have easily done another two hours. I love the energy that comes from a group of people with a shared interest and a common goal. Regardless of what industry you are in, that is when progress happens.

After the workshop, I enjoyed a nice dinner with Dave Ruprecht of *Supermarket Sweep* fame and announcer Randy West. We reminisced about times spent together in Vegas and various other cities and then I made a quick stop by an alumni reunion for former GSN staff members. There were quite a few people there whom I had never met but it was nice to reunite with some folks who had worked with me during *Hollywood Showdown*, *Lover's Lounge* and, of course, *Whammy!*. Many of these people were just starting out in their careers back then and have gone on to some lucrative positions. I'm happy for them and wish them continued success.

At 9:30pm the long day was beginning to take it's toll on me. After returning my rental car, I shuttled back to LAX and checked in for my overnight return flight to Boston. I was exhausted but I could also feel the adrenaline of an extremely productive day pumping through my veins. It was the type of day where people wouldn't believe all you accomplished even if you bothered to tell them. It was the type of day that is filled with opportunity. It was the type of day that I welcome. Less than twenty four hours after crawling out of my own bed I was crawling back into it. I had crossed the country twice, connected and re-connected with some powerful names in the game show industry, and, above it all, had loved every moment of it.

I've had people, mainly girlfriends, occasionally express their disappointment with the fact that I am not a night owl or much of a social butterfly. Fancy parties and events designed to simply be seen hold less than little appeal for me. I think staying out until two in the morning makes no sense. I love my bed, it's the most comfortable bed in the world, and I want to be in it at a normal hour. I don't have to be sleeping, but there's nothing happening on TV, at a bar, or at any party than I'm going to enjoy more than being under those covers. I can promise you that.

Early to bed also means early to rise. Unless I'm on vacation or fighting the flu I do not, cannot, or would not sleep later than 6:30am. My mind takes over and I start thinking about all of the possibilities the new day holds. When this happens, I jump up, workout, and get the machine running.

The great author and speaker Og Mandino wrote in one of his books (I'm almost certain its *The Greatest Salesman In The World,* but you should buy and devour everything that great man ever wrote) "*I will work when failures seek rest,*" and "*Tomorrow is the day reserved for the labor of the lazy.*" When I read Mandino for the first time I was amazed at how insightful he was. His words resonated with me because I've always gone out of my way to look for jobs that others found to be below them. It is a strategy that I share in all of my keynote speeches. Do not pass on *any* opportunity that comes your way because there is *always* something to be gained from it. Maybe the money isn't great but you establish a great contact. Maybe it's a chance to work with someone from whom you can learn a valuable lesson. Or maybe you're not doing anything else that day. Making a little money doing what you love is better than sitting at home and making no money at all. This philosophy has worked in my favor more times than I can remember by allowing me to observe others doing what I wanted to learn how to do, and by opening doors and creating opportunities that otherwise would've gone to someone else who was working a little harder than I was.

Let me give you two examples of when busting my tail has resulted in a major payoff. The first was in the fall 1989. After a semester or three at a community college, I was now attending the University of Missouri-St. Louis (UMSL). On the first day of classes I went straight to the campus radio station and applied for an on air position. The station only played jazz but I didn't care. Today I love its smooth sound, but back then I only wanted to be on air. The station didn't hire me. I didn't even get so much as an interview. I was upset for all of thirty seconds before it dawned on me that they never even asked me if I was a student. It wasn't even a question on the application. This led me to believe that if UMSL didn't care if the people they let on air even went to the school then maybe other colleges would be just as lenient. If that was the case, then every college station within driving distance had just become a target for me. My horizons had expanded greatly as a result of that first rejection.

I had heard of a station at the much smaller Maryville University that played an alternative format and was actually pretty popular with the kids that could pick it up. Because of the station's weak radio tower and signal, this translated to those kids who lived close enough to the school to see the parking lot. I called the station and left a message for the program director. When he returned my call a day or two later he said there was a 1am-4am shift open. Again, no question of my class schedule or if I even knew where the campus was. I asked what day of the week was available and the response was pure gold to me, "Everyday, dude. Nobody wants that shift." Not true. He just hadn't met me yet. I wanted it and I took it. My dad and I struck a deal that gave me access to his car as long as I kept it gassed up for him. Before you could say "*Todd, you're on the air,*" I was on my way to becoming a DJ.

The first station to broadcast my voice on the FM dial was 89.7 KYMC. I knew nothing about alternative music and didn't particularly care for it all that much. I don't even understand the term "alternative." Seems to me that all music would be an alternative to something. I wasn't really interested in learning about the various artists either. I knew enough about Depeche Mode (the lead singer had puked in the OZ bathroom once), Erasure, Concrete Blonde, and a few others to get by.

It really is quite amazing how much experimenting occurs at two in the morning. One entire wall of the studio was filled with vinyl records and I would simply pull and play. If a song struck me as exceptionally weak or seemed to be going on for too long I would just take the needle off the record and play something else. Basically, I was doing what I had done as a kid in my bedroom for years. Playing records just for me and no one else. Little did I know that what audience there actually was at that hour was enjoying this "rebellious" approach. I played deeper tracks than anyone else. One night I even played the entire soundtrack to *Little Shop of Horrors* for no other reason than I liked the few cuts I had heard and wanted to hear the rest of the album.

The radio station was located inside the campus library in a tiny room the size of a broom closet, but it was easily the fanciest digs I had ever seen. I never once complained about the forty minute drive each way. I spent that time listening to the tape of my show from the night before and thinking of ways to improve. The only time I ever raised a fuss was when I'd have to wait for the security guard to unlock the library while I stood outside freezing my cookies off during a midwestern winter. None of it mattered, though. Never once was I late for a shift and I treated each broadcast as if the entire free world was hanging on my every word and dancing wildly to every record I placed on the turntables. Most of this was my own imagination, of course, as the only person who ever called the request line was a guy working at a 7/11. Was I crazy for working the graveyard shift on a low watt radio station for no money? I guess it depends on your definition of crazy. But it was my voice that was heard, if only by a few, and one step always leads to another...and then another.

The next example of doing what others would consider outside the norm is even more memorable to me. I took an internship at HOT 97, a local Top 40 station in St. Louis. The program director, Brian Bridgeman, was not a big fan of mine. He was a young, hot shot PD who had come home to St. Louis after a stint at a station in LA. I was a young kid who was ambitious and got along with everyone at the station because I had a great attitude. Why wouldn't my attitude be great? I was thrilled just to be there.

Brian, who while on the air years earlier in St. Louis used the name "Wild Child," had inherited me from the previous PD, Doc Johnson. Doc was cool, laid back, and just wanted the station to succeed. Brian came in and sold the management on the fact that HOT 97 could and should be number one in the ratings. That was an impossible pitch. Our direct competitor, Q106.5, was strong, legendary in the market, and possessed a signal that reached five times as far as ours did. All of St. Louis tuned into Q106.5 when they wanted to hear the hits. If they tuned into HOT 97 they would most likely hear static. Everyone knew this to be the case, but "Wild Child" presented it well enough to cause a tingling sensation in the corporate britches and they hired him based on fantasy.

As is often the case when a new boss takes over, a few jocks lost their jobs and were replaced by Brian's friends. This is standard practice and radio people, though not always pleased, accept is as par for the course. Brian's team were all good people. Cadillac Jack, Kandy Klutch, and the great Chuck Nasty (who I credit for telling me to "...quit being a pussy and talk into the mic if you want to be on the air.") were the bigger names he brought to town. While they were becoming the new voices of St. Louis, I was folding t-shirts in the prize closet waiting for my shot.

Being an intern is rarely glamorous. That's why today when I meet an intern on a show or at an event I always take a moment to ask them what their plans are for the future and what they've gotten from the experience thus far. I try to share a story or two from my days spent in their shoes. If nothing else, I at least hope they'll realize that sticking with something you're passionate about always pays off in one way or another. They, at the very least, deserve to feel appreciated.

I washed the radio station van, handed out bumper stickers at gas stations, called music stores to find out what music was selling, and gave contest winners directions to the station so they could pick up their prizes. Basically I was there for anything and everything that needed to be done but wasn't worth hiring someone to do.

My enthusiasm didn't go unnoticed. The sales manager, Alice Ross (AJ), soon took notice of my drive and realized that I was a team player. I made no secret about my desire to be on air and she said she was the one to make it happen. Now, AJ is a hard ass but she is smart and definitely someone you want on your side. Truth be told, she was the one who was really running the show back then. Our GM, Michael, was a great guy but he was young and didn't have much experience. Michael's father owned the station and the young up and comer worked hard to learn the ropes and establish himself as a leader. AJ knew the radio game and was the boss behind the boss...and she did not care much for Brian. So let's check our scorecards:

Todd wants to be on the radio.

Wild Child doesn't care for Todd.

AJ likes Todd.

AJ doesn't care for WIld Child.

AJ gets what AJ wants.

How long do you think it took for me to get a shift? The answer is not very long. Within six months I was offered the position of board operator from 3am-6am Monday through Friday. A board op is basically a DJ who isn't allowed to speak. You just press buttons to keep the music playing, make sure all of the commercials run on time, and try to convince the girls who call the request line that you're going to be famous one day. Not the dream gig, but definitely a step closer to it.

After a few months, I was promoted to the entire midnight to 6am shift and received a little bump in pay. I believe that many times we receive great gifts simply because others don't want them. Keeping your eyes open and your head clear gives you the ability to recognize an opportunity when it is presented to you. This is exactly what had occurred with my new overnight shift. I had been trusted with the entire sound of a major market radio station for six hours a day. That's 25% of the broadcast week!

We had a sister station on the AM dial, SOUL 63, that played all Motown music. I knew that I was going to eventually succeed because I was doing the exact *opposite* of what I saw the guys doing on that station. The overnight DJ was a young black guy named Carl. Actually, they were all black guys with that cool cat vibe. All of them were great jocks when they wanted to be. Unfortunately, that wasn't very often. Carl would fall asleep three or four times during an airshift. Instead of preparing for his talk breaks he'd just take the easy way out and play a station ID into the next song. When he would decide to actually speak it would be a lame weather break which he would begin by saying "It's gonna be a great day to wash the car!" He consistently just phoned it in and it infuriated me because I would have walked a mile across broken glass on my ass cheeks for the opportunity that he was tossing away.

My first radio report card. All feedback is good feedback.

I'd watch all of their jocks show up late for their shifts. Many times they'd be smelling of booze or have women in the studio with them. None of them ever offered anything special to their listeners. No unique bits. No content. No personality. They all sounded as if being on the air was keeping them from being with their lovely visitors. I'm not pretending that I never had girls in the studio with me-I often did-but they never detracted from what I did on the air. If anything, they upped my game because I wanted to show off for them. There was one jock in particular who only came to work to get away from his wife, or "The Cheatin' Ho" as he called her. He really despised her. One day he opened his bag to take out his headphones and a pistol fell out onto the floor. I don't think even Dr. Phil could have mended that matrimonial disaster.

Radio stations should be creative environments inhabited by those who wish to entertain through theater of the mind. The guys and girls on SOUL 63 would just read the same promo cards the jock before them had read. It was boring radio...pretty much what you hear today on most terrestrial stations. There's no heart in it. The shining light in this mess is that the experience gave me a chance to see what *not* to do when I finally got on the air. I realized by watching that station sink that if I gave it all I had, even a fraction of what I had, I would one day dominate.

To this day I believe in doing the work others will not do. If the lawn needs to be cut or if there's a leak in the sink I'm going to call someone to take care of that. It's not because I'm lazy. It's because thats not what I do. Chances are I'd screw it up and make the job twice as hard as it needs to be. But if it's something I'm into then I will burn the midnight, morning, noon, late afternoon, early evening, and nighttime oils to make sure I exceed everyone's expectations. Especially my own. That's the only way I've ever known and it works well for me. My dad used to say, "If you're going to do a job, do it right." If things are falling short for you or if you don't feel opportunity has come your way as often as you'd like for it to then perhaps now, *today*, is the time to make a change. Perhaps this is your opportunity to give your life a little more gas, to light a fire under your own tail, and begin to create change.

I would not describe my drive simply as perfectionism or mere determination. I would label it as an *addiction* to perfection and determination. I'm also the first one to admit that I will ditch an idea or project midway through if it loses its purpose. I won't wait around to see if gets better. I'll just move on to something that I *know* is better. It's the old "leave it there the cat will get it" mentality. If you've taken the Restart Profile or been to one of my Restart seminars, then you know this is a definite trait of a Performer. Performers take action...we *need* action. Shoot first ask questions later.

That being said, I do not believe in leaping before you look. I believe every step on your own personal road to greatness should be thought out, structured, and executed with ultimate precision. I just don't think you have to walk around holding a compass or following the stars. That takes too long. I believe in loading your destination into your GPS and getting there as quickly as you can with as few stops as possible. After all, as a wise soul once wrote on the door of a DJ booth in a nightclub I was appearing at, "*The things that come to those who wait are the things left behind by those who got there first.*" That's waxing poetic and I don't need anymore genius than that.

Many times when people ask me how I am doing I'll respond by saying, "Living the dream!" It's obnoxiously upbeat and I intend it to be because generally people don't really care how you or I are doing. They just ask to be polite or as a greeting in passing. My feeling is if you're going to bother asking then I'm going to let you know. I have two great kids. I love my job. I'm in my forties and still have a full head of hair. If that's not the dream then I don't know what is. Going full speed ahead isn't only about working hard in your profession. I believe it's going above and beyond in all areas of your life. It's doing what needs to be done and then some in order to ensure some form of reward or fulfillment. Sometimes that reward comes in the form of money, sometimes it's a few days off to spend with your family. Take whatever comes your way and appreciate it. You've earned it!

Living the dream certainly comes with a price tag. For me, it's spending a lot of time on the road. I travel more than the average bear. I travel more than ten average bears. I'm not bragging nor am I complaining. I'm just stating fact. It's the price of doing business and I'm happy to pay it because I love experiencing the world and I love providing for my kids. Mason and Kiki are my whole world. There is nothing more. I would lay down my life for them without hesitation. It would have to be a pretty good reason, and I'd have to be convinced beyond all doubt that my death was absolutely mandatory for their survival, but I would do it. So, needless to say, I would also do anything in my power to spend every possible moment with them.

Silver, their mother and my ex-wife, is an incredible lady. We're not married anymore, but I believe I found the perfect woman to give me children and to have as their mother for all of their lives. Being married for seven and a half years was just a part of the master plan. I am grateful to her for my babies. Any man who does not appreciate what a woman goes through emotionally, hormonally, and physically during pregnancy and childbirth is just a self absorbed monster. I may have appeared unappreciative plenty of times in my life, but not when it comes to my kids or my family. Silver is not only a fabulous mother but she understands the vital role a father plays in a child's life and works hard to accommodate my schedule so that I get as much time with my angels as possible.

I fell for Silver in December of 1999. At the time, she was assistant to one of the E! executives. She was hard to miss. Her long blonde hair and beautiful blue eyes were the only reasons I needed to find an excuse to walk past her desk on a daily basis. I knew the first time I kissed her that there would be no turning back. It would be full speed ahead or nothing at all.

I asked her to move in with me in January of 2000, proposed in February, we got married in July, and were pregnant with Mason in October. I know...wow! Pretty fast, huh? In her defense, that pace was set by me and I'm not sure she was ever that comfortable with it. You'd have to ask her. It was probably too fast and the fact that we never took the time to build a foundation may have been a contributing factor to our divorce. For those who still consider a divorce to be some sort of failure, I disagree and make no apologies. That's just how our story unfolded. Everything has a beginning and an end. "Full speed ahead" is how I'm programmed to do things. It is who I am and I'm not looking to change. I share these stories with you to show that, overall, this modus operandi has led to great joy in all areas of my life.

Gene Simmons from KISS is someone I have great admiration for. Not only because I'm a card carrying member of the KISS Army, but because he is a thinker and a doer. He's also a gentleman. One evening at a 2001 fundraiser for MDA at the Beverly Hilton Hotel in Beverly Hills, I took Silver over to Gene's table to say hello. He was just diving into his desert but took the time to put down his fork, stand up from the table, and shake her hand. Class act.

The band's overwhelming and long lasting success is due mainly to Gene's creativity, vision, and business sense. In his book *Sex, Lies and KISS*, the demon shares many of his philosophies on everything from marriage to lovemaking. It's a great read and I highly recommend it. Gene says that we are all given the same amount of hours in the day. It's how we choose to fill them that separates the winners from the losers. I choose to sleep a little less than others so I have more time to play with my kids, keep my body and mind strong, and create ways to make money. There are a lot of dollars floating around out there and I want as many of them to end up in my wallet as possible. I also want to see and do as many interesting and memorable things as possible. Next week, for example, I'll begin an eight week run of *The Price Is Right Live!* in Atlantic City. After Saturday's show I'll hop a bus to New York City in order to emcee the nation's largest pet adoption fair on Sunday morning. After making sure as many of our furry friends find loving homes as we can, I'll catch a bus back to AC for two shows that afternoon and evening. Again, not complaining. I want the animals to find families, I want to entertain the boardwalk audience, and I want to earn a paycheck. If you have a better idea of how to achieve that in a twenty four hour period then please email me and share your wisdom.

Every single morning that you open your eyes to find your heart is still beating is an opportunity to move full speed ahead and make a difference. Why not give it all you've got? Being passionate and hungry is not a crime. Our government does not make it easy to chase the shooting star with business taxes, endless paperwork, and other forms of red tape, but it does make it *possible.* Vision is what this country was founded upon. If my words don't convince you, I encourage you to read some books on our founding fathers. They were fascinating men who risked it all in pursuit of a dream. Without vision, motivation, and the drive to follow a dream with all of your heart what good are you to anyone? Your family deserves more. Your industry deserves more. *You* deserve more.

Close your eyes for a moment and envision your life playing on one of those old television sets that has knobs below the screen to adjust color, contrast, and volume. When you see yourself on the screen- when you *really* see yourself-I want you to reach down and turn those knobs. Crank em up! Make the picture *bigger, brighter, and louder*! Now focus on how that makes you feel physically. Isn't it exciting? Can you feel the rush running up your spine? Sometimes you need to do it three or four times to get yourself into that excited state but it's worth it. This is a popular NLP exercise we do at my seminars and you can just feel the increase in energy it produces when people really get into it. That internal excitement is yours for the taking. No fear. No limits. Find what motivates you, break down a few barriers, and go full speed ahead *now.*

CHAPTER 5
IT'S WHO YOU KNOW

Television is an invention that lets you be entertained in your living room by people you wouldn't have in your home.
-David Frost

THE FIRST VIDEO EVER played on MTV was *Video Killed The Radio Star* by the British new wave band, The Buggles. That was a bold and courageous choice. By playing that particular song at a time when the network knew the entire country was watching, MTV made the statement, *"We're going to give this all we've got. Get on board or get out of the way."*

The concept of playing videos all day long was a huge risk for a new network looking to establish itself with advertisers and viewers. Many in the world of television asked, "Why would people turn on their TVs just to listen to music?" Clearly that risk paid off and the channel, now seen worldwide, changed the music industry forever.

Video Killed The Radio Star threw all of MTV's cards on the table and acknowledged that artists who have enjoyed success on radio may or may not have the crossover appeal needed to make it on the small screen. In other words, some are better off only being heard and not seen. This not only applies to singers and bands, but also to a lot of radio personalities.

DJs are a rare breed. Many of us who were vaccinated at birth with phonograph needles have what is often referred to as "a face for radio." As a result, some jocks prefer to lock themselves away in their acoustically controlled environments and simply hide behind the microphone. They are loners who enjoy talking *to* the masses-not *with* the masses. I'm the opposite. I'm certain that much of my success with radio request line groupies stemmed solely from the fact that they were just relieved to find I wasn't three hundred pounds and bald when they met me. I'm pretty sure this fact also contributed to the high number of personal appearances I was booking. Whatever the case, I was planning to surf the lucrative airwaves until I hit the sandy beaches of fame and fortune or the hard dirt of the radio graveyard. Whichever came first.

In 1991, the local FOX affiliate in St. Louis asked if I'd be interested in appearing in a public service announcement that would run during *Beverly Hills 90210. 90210* was the most popular show on television at the time and the station wanted to air a "Don't Drink & Drive" campaign coinciding with the upcoming prom season. This was a huge opportunity for some great exposure and since I was the number one rated DJ with teens, and *90210* was the number one show with anyone with a pulse, it was the perfect fit. I thought back to when I was a kid listening to the radio up in my room and imagining what the DJs looked like. Giving people a chance to put a face to the voice would instantly strengthen the connection I had with my listeners, introduce me to tens of thousands who had never heard of me, associate me with their favorite TV show, and attach me to a wonderful cause. This was a win all the way around.

I agreed and showed up at the station a few days later. I brought only one outfit with me. Normally, when supplying your own wardrobe, the producers request that you bring a few "choices." I have never brought more than two "choices" because then I am guaranteed to wear something that *I* feel comfortable in and not something that a stylist whom I've never met concocts for me. I knew what I looked good in and, even more importantly, I knew how I wanted the teens to see me. Even though it was the middle of summer, I broke out my leather biker jacket and my favorite pair of jeans. It was all about the image and this was *not* the image most of the viewers were used to when it came to radio personalities. I needed to make an impact in order to break myself from the stereotype and this was just the outfit to do it in.

Ruling the St. Louis airwaves as Rick Idol. 1992.

There were no protests from the producers. In fact, I think they just wanted to get me in and out of there as quickly as possible so they could get a dinner break before the evening news broadcast. The makeup artist powdered me down to make sure I wasn't shiny underneath the studio lights and I took my position in front of the camera. The crew had marked my spot with an X made of green tape. I looked down to check my footing then looked back up to check the teleprompter.

Seeing my name in the script was a thrill for me. I had never read a teleprompter before and instantly realized what a great invention it was. The producer had faxed me a copy of the script the night before which I took to mean that I was expected to have it all memorized by the time I came in. It wasn't that much copy and most of it was saying who I was and encouraging kids to choose a designated driver. Even though I'd rehearsed it a hundred times on the drive over, I was thankful the prompter was there as a backup. Like we always say in TV...never refuse a breath mint or a cue card!

The stage manager was an older gentleman who had worked at the station for many years. The volume on his headset was cranked up to an obscenely loud level and I overheard the director say we had speed, which means we were recording. He counted down from three to one and pointed at me. This was my cue to let it fly.

I had so much information in my head that the words came out rapid fire. I spoke way too quickly. This was partially due to nerves and partially due to my desire to be perfect. A second take was called for and I was given the note to talk to the camera as if I was taking into the radio microphone. I just needed to relax. This was good advice and it led to us getting the perfect take on just the second time out.

My plea for teens to choose a designated driver came from a very real place. I had lost a high school friend in an automobile accident. When a life is taken at such a young age it affects everyone. If this PSA could make an impact, and possibly save a life, I wanted it to hit the mark.

Knowing we had a great one "in the can," we went ahead and did a few more just to drive it home. This is where I played with the copy a little. I grew more and more comfortable with each take and, when I saw the finished product for the first time, I was proud of what we had done.

I milked it for all that it was worth as soon as the commercial began airing. I gave prizes to the first people who called in to the station after seeing it. I would only put callers on the air who had rave things to say. Mostly young girls. FOX had given me a schedule of when it was going to run so I worked the airings into my radio show.

A local director for the D.A.R.E. organization caught wind of it and asked me if I would be willing to take part in their school assembly presentations. The plan was for a police officer and me to visit local high schools and talk about making wise choices. Adults aren't fools. As much as we wish it weren't the case, we know kids are going to experiment with alcohol, cigarettes, maybe even drugs. Personally, I've always believed the way to combat these vices is to arm young people with massive amounts of self esteem.

When I would take the stage I wouldn't waste time talking about how smoking causes cancer. I'm no doctor and everyone already knows the health risks involved. I would talk about how some people in that very auditorium, on that very day, were going to grow up to become rich. Some may become pro athletes. Someone may even become President. I let them know, at that particular moment in time, that they all had the very same chance for a great life. What would ultimately make the difference and allow some to swim while others sink, are the choices they would make now and in the future. Holding yourself in high regard leads to wise choices. Wise choices lead to productive behavior. That type of behavior leads to positive outcomes. I preached it then and I preach it now. The opposite is also true. If you don't respect yourself enough to make the right choices when it comes to what you put in your body and your mind, the results will be disappointing.

I would end each presentation by saying, "The choice is yours. You have that power right now and, whether you realize it or not, you are surrounded by people who believe in you. I am one of those people. Thanks so much and make sure you tune in to my show tonight so I can talk about how awesome this school is!"

*Working a high school crowd into a frenzy
for the D.A.R.E organization. 1992.*

The crowd would erupt! I've always scanned the audience when I've given any kind of presentation. The eyes will reveal how deep of an impact you're making. If the audience, especially teenagers, is fidgeting around and whispering to each other you don't have them where you want them. You probably don't have them at all. Teens are the toughest group to engage. It's not perceived as "cool" to be captivated by a speaker.

Another obstacle you face is that they have nothing invested in your presentation. When I speak today, it's usually to an audience who has paid money to see me. They *want* to take something away from our time together so they will be present and attentive. A typical high school student is just happy to be out of class and really couldn't care less about what you have to say unless you strike a specific chord. But when every eye is one you and it's so quiet that you can hear a mouse fart, you know you're connecting on a very deep level. That's an incredible feeling. That seemed to be the case with every school we visited. The kids not only listened to what I had to say but would follow me out to the radio station van like I was Luke Perry.

Many times the pandemonium these assemblies led to was more than the school faculty had ever been exposed to so I started bringing a friend of mine along to serve as security. He called himself "Tricky T" and was a local rap artist with dread locks and tattoos. Things never got rough or out of hand, but having Tricky there helped maintain order and added to the superstar image. My ratings were climbing and I was appearing all over town. More appearances meant more money. The momentum was powerful and it seemed to all be due to television. I wanted more.

I wasn't the only one enjoying success on the airwaves. The station, Q106.5, was doing very well as a whole. We had a strong morning team, Steve & DC, and a great afternoon personality named Kenny Knight. We all appreciated what was going on and, as I'd learned with the Wizards of OZ, when the team is winning everyone benefits.

Things hit a serious snag when one of the morning hosts made a racial slur that caused a big stir throughout the entire city. DC Chymes was the culprit and, almost overnight, our bright and sunny radio station was stuck under the darkest of clouds.

It was a careless, immature, and unprofessional comment that should not have been made by a professional broadcaster in any market, big or small. There is no excuse for anyone to use the term that DC used. It's never funny and it hurt more people than just the woman he intended it for.

As a result of what was said, the station lost advertisers and threats of violence were called in to the station. At one point we even had police officers posted outside. I'll admit it was a little scary, especially for me. Most people left the station at 5pm, whereas I had to be there alone until midnight.

While Steve and DC attended anger management classes and tried to restore their image (a.k.a. save their jobs) I began focusing on myself and my show. As far as I was concerned, those guys were on their own. They'd both been around long enough to be held accountable. I felt bad that Steve had been drawn into it, but he chose to stick by his partner and ride the storm out as a team. I admired him for that.

I decided to make Rick Idol an entity unto itself. People had a bad taste in their mouths when it came to our radio station so I held off on mentioning the call letters when I went out on appearances. I made it all about the party and the prizes. I gave away as much as I could so people would begin to associate me with good times and winning rather than the negativity brought on by my colleague. Fortunately Q106.5 did more live appearances than any other station in the market so I had plenty of opportunities to get out of the studio and onto the street where people could see me and be a part of the action.

Every Sunday night, we would broadcast my show live from a nightclub in Illinois called Stagez. The place was initially just an old warehouse that put on rock shows and sold cheap beer, but a young guy named Milan Venezia realized its potential and bought it for a song. He completely revamped the place and put in a multi level dance floor, a new sound system, and spent barrels of money to advertise on our station.

Everyone who has ever been to a nightclub knows that men go there to meet women. Women go there to dance and have men buy them drinks. It always has been and always will be that way. Everyone also knows that men love watching young women dance. Thus the more young women you have dancing the more men you will have watching and buying alcohol at a huge markup. Milan made Stagez open to girls 18 and over. Men had to be 21. I'm not sure if that was legal, but no one ever said anything. Within a month the place was slammed with hot girls and drooling chumps. The music played until 6am and the money was rolling in hand over fist.

Milan and I had a great relationship that got better and better as the club grew more and more successful. He took care of me financially and I spoke of Stagez nonstop on my radio show. I would put callers on the air to talk about what a great time they'd had at the club. It eventually got to the point where cars would be lined up on the side of the freeway just to get in. The line to get through the front door surpassed anything I'd ever seen at OZ and, to be honest, rivaled anything I've seen since at Disneyland. Many times I'd bring the microphone outside and talk to people waiting to get in. To those listening on the radio, there was no doubt Stagez was where you wanted to be and at the center of it all was Rick Idol.

Drivers crossing the Mississippi River into Illinois could not miss the giant Stagez/Rick Idol billboard.

The club reeked of stale beer, cheap hairspray, and opportunity. While three thousand people were dancing, drinking, and making out in any dark corner they could find, I was thinking of ways to make this even bigger. My audience was a healthy mix of all ethnicities and they seemed to be letting go of the Steve & DC mess. Or, at the very least, they didn't see me as part of it. When we would go off the air at Stagez, I would do a contest or two like we used to do at The OZ. As soon as I said goodnight on the radio, a massive rush of bodies would make its way to the front of the stage. I can't explain it. I know a lot of radio people and none of them have ever experienced anything quite like it. What we had at Q106.5 and Stagez was unique to the time. It was so very special. I needed to capitalize on it and I had a pretty good idea of how I was going to do it.

Milan's father, Tom, was the money man behind the whole operation. My idea involved a TV producer friend of mine named Scott Wibbenmeyer. Scott and I set up a meeting with Tom at his office in Belleville, IL. He was all too happy to listen to our proposal. Stagez was doing phenomenal business and he had money to burn, so Scott and I presented him with the concept of a local dance video show-our own version of *American Bandstand*. We already had a great location and the people. All we needed was a camera crew and a place to air the show. Scott handled the technical side. He laid out exactly what we would need and how much it would cost. I suggested, since Tom had deep pockets, that he buy infomercial time on KPLR Channel 11 rather than try to sell the show. This way we would be in complete control and not find ourselves smothered by having too many cooks in the kitchen. He loved the idea!

One thing I always liked about Tom was that he didn't waste any time. This is a common trait among achievers. They never seem to let too much grass grow under their expensive Italian loafers. He called the TV station shortly after our meeting and purchased a key time slot. Thursday nights at midnight, right after *Baywatch*. Tom didn't realize it, but *Baywatch* was the biggest show in the world at that time and to have it as our lead in was more than we could have ever hoped for. Scott went to work on assembling a crew and we scheduled the first tape date for the following Sunday.

In keeping with the tradition set forth by great self promoters like P.T. Barnum, Houdini, Dick Clark, Gene Simmons, and Johnny Carson, I wanted to have my name in the show's title. Repetition builds reputation. Tom didn't object, and *Live at Stages with Rick Idol* was born.

When I returned to the radio the following Monday night, I teased the new show every time I popped on the microphone. I said I had a huge announcement exclusively for my listeners. It was something they would *not* want to miss. Hide your babies and lock up your old ladies because this was going to be big! The phone lines were buzzing with people wanting an inside scoop. I wouldn't give even the tiniest of hints. Finally, at 9pm when I knew the prime time network TV shows were over and the most people were tuned in, I let the cat out of the bag.

"Rick Idol has your chance to be a FEATURED dancer on a hot, new show being taped right here in St. Louis!"

I told people if they've always dreamed of being on television then they had to be at Stagez that Sunday afternoon dressed to impress and ready dance. It was all I talked about all week long. My program director begged me to promote other things going on at the station but his hands were pretty much tied because, at the time, Stagez was our biggest advertiser. I milked it for all it was worth.

On the Sunday that we were scheduled to shoot, even though the sun was still up, the Stagez parking lot was overflowing. Inside we pumped up the music and just let the people do their thing.

Milan and his girlfriend walked around and picked out ten guys and ten girls to be our "featured dancers." We paid them $25 a show to basically be our insurance that we'd always have good looking people to point the cameras at if needed.

My friends from various record companies sent me boxes of music videos to use on the show. Most of it was from artists no one had ever heard of. We rarely featured a hit song but it never seemed to matter. As long as there was a beat people would be moovin' and groovin', shakin' and bakin'. That's all we wanted and since we paid for the airtime we weren't concerned with ratings. It was all one giant commercial for Stagez...and for me.

No one will work harder for you than *you*. No one. Ever. Surrounding yourself with the best employees, partners, lawyers, web designers, and accountants will certainly propel you further than if you choose the wrong associates or to go it alone, but when it comes to taking care of *you* we all know who's shoulders the responsibility falls upon.

I was dating a girl named Nikki during this time. Nikki was, and is, a massively talented girl. She sings, dances, acts, and does it all very well. Though a few years younger than me, she was unusually patient and tolerant. It could not have been easy to be with me back then. I was working every weeknight until midnight and every weekend until the early morning hours. She'd occasionally visit me at the radio station and hear the girls calling on the request lines. Through it all, I stayed faithful. I've never been one to hurt someone I truly care for, but sometimes a woman's perception can be more painful than reality.

Nikki had short dark hair and the warmest, most beautiful brown eyes. I saw a future every time I looked into them and wasn't going to let what happened with Kelly happen with us. I also felt very much at home with Nikki's family. It was a tight, loving group and I always enjoyed attending pool parties, dinners, and get togethers with them.

Back then, Nikki was a member of a group of young people who did vignettes that aired during KPLR's afternoon cartoons. The woman in charge of them was named Lois and I knew her only from those occasions where I'd come pick Nikki up from a shoot.

I phoned Lois and told her I had a proposition she might be interested in. Obviously, Nikki and her cohorts were popular with the little kids, but what about the teens? The station didn't have a face that demographic could identify with and, with KPLR's new affiliation with Six Flags theme park, there was potential for all types of programming that would be appealing to them. Lois ran it up the flagpole and I was called in to speak with the station owner, Ted Koplar.

Ted is a unique character. You never really felt like you had his full attention. Not because he wasn't interested, but rather because he had the attention span of a kitten. Shiny things caught his eye and you really had to work to bring him back to the conversation. Our meeting was pretty cut and dry. Ted knew before I even showed up that he was going to hire to me.

In addition to seasonal specials from the Six Flags theme park, KPLR brought me aboard to host a talk show geared towards teens called *Workin' It Out*. Not only did the KPLR contract double my annual income, but I was now doubling my exposure in St. Louis and gathering more and more material for my radio show.

Representing KPLR at a fundraiser for Children's Miracle Network. 1994.

The Six Flags shows were a lot of fun, but I don't think anyone over the legal voting age ever tuned in to watch them. *Workin' It Out* was a bit more successful. We did two episodes. Both featured a live studio audience of local high school students discussing topics like violence, drugs and alcohol, and community involvement.

With each new project I was learning more and more about television production as well as developing my interviewing skills. Although I enjoyed the writing and editing process, I came to realize that in front of the camera is where I belonged. It is just as important to know your weaknesses as it is to know your strengths and there were people working on our shows that were very strong in areas where I was not. Thomas Gibson and Tom Bellos, both dear friends with whom I would later work with at E!, served as the show's producers and did a fine job with what they had to work with. Watching them constantly putting out fires and handling all the odds and ends led to my decision to focus solely on being talent. I knew I had the goods and now I also had some experience under my belt. It was time for that next step. The only problem was I had no idea what that next step would be.

After *Workin' It Out*, KPLR seemed to have run out of things to do with me. You can only make so many shows about roller coasters and log flumes. I didn't hear from the station for several weeks. With only a few months remaining on my one year contract, a woman named Sandy Miller gave me a call. She had just been hired in the promotions department and was full of fresh ideas. One of which included me in a big way. She called it *IdolWear*.

Sandy wanted to produce a new clothing line featuring my name. She had a proposal, which I signed without reading, that included t-shirts and hats to be sold at local outlets around town. The shirts came in black or white. The hats were a different story. They came in two styles, revolting and hideous. Didn't matter. When the shirts arrived I started giving them away on my radio show. We set up appearances at the malls and even shot a TV commercial that featured Nikki and my brand new Pontiac Firebird. Sales were strong and word of mouth spread like cold sores. People showed up at Stagez in their *IdolWear*. I'd see kids at the mall in their *IdolWear*. Parents were stopping by the radio station on their lunch breaks to pick up some *IdolWear* for their teenagers. It was a hit.

Truth be told, I ended up never seeing a dime from *IdolWear*, but every radio trade publication ran a story on the shirts and that PR was worth much more to me than a couple of small checks. I felt like I had it all. So much so that I began to grow concerned there wasn't much more to be had. I was starting to outgrow the city I had grown up in.

KPLR had become the local WB affiliate in St. Louis. The WB was getting ready to launch several new sitcoms on their stations across the country and KPLR assigned me to host the junkets out in Los Angeles. For those who may not know, a junket is where a bunch of reporters gather in one hotel to interview the stars of an upcoming movie or TV series. You get anywhere from 5 to 10 minutes to ask all of your questions and hopefully get some good soundbites to use in the finished story. When you see a local entertainment reporter laughing and messing around with a major star while they sit in director's chairs in front of a movie poster, you know it's a junket.

The more junkets I did for KPLR, and eventually for E!, the more I came to feel sorry for the stars. Sure, they get paid a lot of money for doing what they do and schmoozing the press is part of the job, but listening to one geeky interviewer after another ask you the same questions over and over must get exhausting. I don't know how they do it. I, of course, said I'd be thrilled to fly to Hollywood and be KPLR's geeky interviewer. It would, at the very least, get my face on the evening news alongside Bobcat Goldthwait.

I've talked quite a bit about defining moments in one's life and how recognizing opportunity is key when pursuing your dreams. Notice I use the word *pursuing* rather than *chasing* when I refer to your dreams. The reason I do this is simple-your dreams don't run away from you. There is nothing to chase. They are right there for the taking. Achieving what you want to achieve is simply a matter of doing what needs to be done in order to grab the golden cookie. There are no shortcuts. Success is a series of seized opportunities. You never really know when those opportunities are going to come your way but you are fully aware when one passes you by. The trick is to never look in your rearview mirror with regret. Keep your eyes pointed at the horizon and nothing will slip through the cracks.

My eyes were certainly wide open while I was in Hollywood. I had only been to Los Angeles once before. FOX Television did a promotion with several radio stations and flew some DJs out to L.A. to be extras on the show *Living Single* with Queen Latifa. Still, there was a certain excitement in the air on this trip as the wheels of my plane touched down at LAX. The station had a car service waiting for me outside and I made my way to the Universal Sheraton in Universal City.

I was scheduled to interview the Wayons Brothers, Shawn and Marlon, that afternoon. For one reason or another, Marlon had to cancel and I found myself with some time to kill. As I stood at my hotel room window looking out over the San Fernando Valley, I noticed the address on the building next door. It was the MTV building and I recognized it from when I sent in an audition tape for the show *Real World* the year before. At that time everyone wanted to be on *Real World* and I was no exception.

Fortunately, I was prepared. Any good radio guy knows you never go anywhere without a copy of your demo tape. You never know who you are going to bump into. I once slipped my demo tape into Casy Casem's luggage while giving him a ride to the airport. Casey had stopped by our radio station to promote his countdown show and I thought I'd give it a shot. He called me later to thank me for the lift and had kind words to say about my on air performance. That was a huge boost for me.

Now that my sights were set more on television I never went anywhere, certainly not to Hollywood, without a VHS tape of my TV work. It wasn't great but it was a solid four minutes of material from Stagez, Six Flags, and *Workin' It Out* that I could be proud of. Hopefully the people at MTV would be as taken with it as I was.

Call it youthful courage or just plain naiveté, but whatever it was, something lured me out of the hotel and over to MTV's offices. Once I located the main reception area, I walked up to the young lady behind the desk and asked, "Can you please direct me to the person I would speak to about becoming a VJ?"

Now, normally I would have been tossed right out of the building. You just don't do that kind of thing but at the time I didn't think twice about it. There I was, a twenty two year old disc jockey from Missouri with little more than a demo tape and a dream.

Sporting an assortment of hair colors, multiple piercings in each ear, and tattoos peeking out from the bottom of her sleeves, the woman behind the circular counter was exactly what you would expect in terms of an MTV hire. She smiled and politely told me to have a seat as she reached for the phone. I expected security to arrive at any moment to haul me away.

Instead, a man who introduced himself as Curt Sharp appeared and led me down a long hallway to his office. The walls were decorated with signed posters of every rock band known to man. I sat down in a guest chair while he took a seat behind his desk. He listened intently as I gave him the short version of my background and the long version of why I would be a great VJ. To me, it seemed like the next logical step in my career. I knew what was hot in music, had a great voice, and a head of highlighted hair just like Adam Curry's.

Curt took the time to watch my tape and said he liked what he saw. The next step, he told me, would be finding representation. I had no idea what he was talking about. Up until that point I did all of my own legwork when it came to finding gigs and honestly didn't even realize there were agents and managers who do that type of thing for you. In an effort to jump this hurdle and keep the meeting moving forward, I asked Curt if there was anyone he could recommend who might be interested in me. After thinking about it for a moment, he picked up his phone and made three calls.

The first agent he called wasn't taking on any new clients, certainly not a no name from nowhere with no experience. The second call he made was to a well known hosting agent named Babette Perry. Babette is successful at what she does because she is always on the lookout for fresh talent. She instructed Curt to send my tape over so that she could have a look at it. That was definitely a step in the right direction, but I only had one tape to give and Curt still had one call to make.

His third and final call was to Nicole Taylor. A fresh, new agent at an agency called Abrams, Rubaloff and Lawrence, Nicole had been Babette's assistant and was now branching out on her own. A,R,&L represented some big names in hosting at that time. People like Bob Goen of *ET*, Marc Summers of *Double Dare,* and many others. So far it seemed like a good match.

The southern California stars must have been aligned for me that day because Nicole informed Curt that her lunch meeting had just cancelled and if I'd like to come right over she'd be happy to meet with me. Even if I would have had something planned for that afternoon there is no doubt in my mind I would've blown it off to meet with Nicole. The problem was I had no idea where I was going. Curt wrote down the address and told me where I could catch a cab. He said the quickest route would be to go over "the hill," which is the mountain that separates the Valley from the rest of Los Angeles. There are a few ways to go over it, Laurel Canyon, Coldwater Canyon, Beverly Glen, and just about any of them would be quicker than taking a freeway.

I only had $100 in my wallet and that had to last me for the whole trip. I had no idea how long of a drive it was, but I knew I could figure all of that out later. If I found myself short of cash I could always call the hotel and hopefully someone would come fetch me. It's not like I'd be the first guy with big dreams to find himself broke in the big city. L.A. must have a rescue plan set up for that sort of thing. As a matter of fact it does. It's called the public bus system.

As we drove down Ventura Boulevard and over Laurel Canyon I had to remind myself to maintain my composure in spite of what was happening all around me. There were no cell phones back then otherwise I'm sure I would've been calling everyone I knew to tell them what was going on. Instead I just rode in silence, staring out the taxi window as we passed mansion after mansion on the winding canyon road.

My excitement grew as we crossed over Hollywood Boulevard and eventually the Sunset Strip. I had never experienced this part of Hollywood before and could tell almost immediately that it had a much different vibe from the Valley. The Laugh Factory, Rainbow Room, and Mondrian Hotel were places I had only seen on television but were now within a stone's throw. The outdoor restaurants and coffee shops were packed with young, beautiful people who clearly spent way too much money on clothing designed to make them look as if they'd spent very little. I'm sure if you searched every one of them, at least half would have a glossy headshot stashed somewhere on their person. This was where things happened, you could just feel it.

It's almost surreal when you find yourself in a place you've only heard or read about. Much like the Vegas strip, the Grand Canyon, or Niagra Falls, Hollywood had been little more than a fairytale land to me. We continued driving north past boutiques and office buildings of modern decor until finally the cab came to a stop. I looked down at the piece of paper Curt had given me and up at the address on the building. This was the place. The fare came to $40. I tipped the driver a five spot and smiled, knowing that things had worked out once again. I'd have more than enough cash to get back.

I tapped my foot nervously as I waited in the reception area of the second floor office. Not knowing what to expect and reluctant to get my hopes up too high, I remained cautiously optimistic. I was soon escorted back into Nicole's office by Amy, an executive assistant who's beauty rivaled that of any modern day starlet. You see that a lot in Los Angeles. Everyone steps off the bus with dreams of lighting up the silver screen but soon realizes there are a few steps between leaving home and seeing your name on the marquee. Those who are fortunate enough to land a job at a talent agency are certainly on the right track.

Nicole was younger than I expected but just as friendly as she could be. We had an instant rapport and I could see she felt just as comfortable with me as I did with her. My earlier meeting with Curt had given me a chance to perfect my pitch. When Nicole asked me to tell her about myself I was crisp and concise. I told her exactly what my career had consisted of to that point and why I was ready to move forward.

I've been in hundreds of meetings where everyone in attendance is just blowing hot air at each other. This was not one of those meetings. There was a real connection. If someone is going to be taking 10% of your pre-taxed earnings, you definitely want it to be someone you can hold a conversation with. Nicole told me that in order for an agent/talent relationship to work there had to be a mutual trust and respect. I had to trust that she would represent me in a way that was in my best interest and she had to respect that it was my career she was holding in her hands. At that point in my life, before my kids, nothing was more important to me than my career.

After thirty minutes of chit chat and feeling each other out, Nicole took me in to meet her boss, Richard Lawrence. Richard is well known in the non-scripted television genre. He has successfully packaged and sold a long list of projects and personally represents an impressive roster of talent. I liked him and he liked me. After a firm handshake and a "nice to meet you" or two, Nicole and I returned to her office and she went for the close. She slapped her hands on top of her desk and said she'd like to represent me. I couldn't believe it. I woke up that morning thinking that the day would consist of nothing more than getting a photo taken with a couple of guys who used to be on *In Living Color,* and now here I was with a real Hollywood agent offering to sign me. Anyone who tells you that Hollywood is not the city where dreams come true hasn't spent enough time there.

Things were moving so fast. For some reason still unknown to me, I thought I needed to slow it all down a bit. I told Nicole I needed a day or two to process everything and would call her when I returned home. This may sound like some sort of negotiating ploy but it was nothing of the sort. I had nothing to negotiate. I needed an agent if I was ever going to get anywhere and here one was sitting right before me. Moving too quickly would have serious consequences, however, and I needed to let it breathe. Nicole understood and told me to call her when I was ready. The lovely assistant Amy called me a cab and saw me to the front door.

The next morning I boarded my TWA flight bound for St. Louis. Nikki picked me up from the airport and we had a quick dinner before driving back to my apartment. I told her about the whole trip and she couldn't believe all that had transpired in just 72 hours. We always supported each other in our careers but I could tell she was a little concerned about what may happen next and what it would mean for us as a couple. Trying to comfort her was difficult because I knew in the back of my mind, if the opportunity arose, I would have to roll the dice and move out west. There was no question I had strong feelings for her. Walking away from our relationship would be difficult, but I still had many mountains yet to climb.

When we got home I went to clean out my mailbox. After three days there was plenty of junk mail to be tossed. Among the grocery ads and credit card offers was an overnight envelope with a California postmark. I immediately opened it. Nicole had sent the agency papers for me to sign along with a handwritten note.

Ready when you are...
Nicole

I tucked the papers in my bag. Nikki seeing them would only have resulted in an all night discussion that neither one of us was prepared to have. I just wanted to go to bed. After Nikki left for her classes the next morning, I signed the papers and overnighted them back to Nicole. I called her office as soon as it opened and thanked her for having faith in me.

Nicole and I spoke for nearly an hour. She told me about the opportunities available at the moment and how I might fit in to the current trends in television. I told her I was up for just about anything but I refused to quit my job and move to California without a solid gig. I had too good of a thing going to throw it all away on wing and a prayer. We agreed that I would come to LA once a month for meetings and auditions. If something really big popped up, or if Nicole had a hunch about a particular project, I had to trust her enough to fly myself out there and follow up on it. It seemed fair enough and I had plenty of Stagez money stashed away. I assured her the travel costs and the time off from work wouldn't be a problem.

During those first monthly visits, I think I met just about every casting agent in town. I auditioned for reality shows, game shows, talk shows, basically any show that didn't involve acting. Maury Povich saw something in me and signed me for a pilot. It was a talk show called *The Village* along with two female co-hosts, Maiquel Suarez and Lynn Blades. They were a dream to work with but, unfortunately, the last thing the country needed at that time was another daytime talk show and our project didn't get picked up.

To ease the blow, Nicole took me out for sushi the night before I was scheduled to fly home. She told me she had a last minute audition for me early the next morning. If I was up for it, I could swing by and meet with E! Entertainment Television before my flight. It would be a tight squeeze but I could make it work.

Dan Gibson was the well known talent coordinator for E! in those days. Everyone who has ever met Dan absolutely loves him. He told me they were looking for someone to host a movie preview show called *Coming Attractions*. Nothing too exciting or difficult. Basically it required the host to sit on a stool and introduce a bunch of movie trailers. All of the copy was on teleprompter and I could pretty much read it at my own pace. I had become quite proficient with a teleprompter at KPLR so I knew it wouldn't be a problem.

The E! studio was nothing like the KPLR studio. That would be like comparing a tricycle to a Harley Davidson. This was the big time. The first thing I remember seeing was the purple *Talk Soup* chair. Greg Kinnear had just left to pursue an acting career and John Henson (Skunkboy) was making quite a name for himself as the new host. Steve Kmetko and Kathleen Sullivan were the anchors for E! News and

I saw the stools they used for their daily broadcast stashed away in the corner to make room for my green screen. Dan introduced me to the crew, who had met dozens of hosts during this audition process, then took me into makeup.

The makeup artist was beautiful young woman named Jeannette. More than beautiful, she was stunning. I definitely wasn't in St. Louis anymore. Jeannette started applying bronzer, concealer, eyeliner, and powder to my face. She could have painted me up like Bozo the Clown and I wouldn't have minded. I was in E!'s hands at that point. Speaking of hands, my palms started to sweat from a combination of doing the biggest audition of my life and Jeannette's face coming within inches of mine in the makeup chair. The Hollywood scene would take some getting used to, but I was ready to take it on.

I returned to the studio and took my position in front of the green screen. The crew, even though they had been doing this all day, still gave me their full attention. They are a fabulous group. Tommy Mac, Alan Wu, Cynthia Malone, Fred Mendes, I recognized all of them from their cameos on *Talk Soup*. The atmosphere was light and fun, the way I wish all sets could be. I was instantly at ease and it came across. The audition was a piece of cake. We did it twice and I was more than satisfied with both takes.

I hightailed it to the airport and called Nicole from a pay phone to tell her that I felt it went really well. A week later, E! called her office and offered me a job.

The offer was straightforward. It was a four year deal and I would host *Coming Attractions*, provide all of the voiceovers for the network, and be available for anything else they needed me to do. The money was what we needed it to be and then some. Nicole was happy with all of the terms so we accepted. I was bursting with excitement. This is exactly what I had been working for. But now came the difficult part. I had to tell Nikki, my parents, and the radio station. First, Mom and Dad.

I invited my parents to join me at a little Mexican restaurant in south St. Louis. Both were a tad suspicious when I called them out of the blue and asked them to dinner. My mother can be a bit of a worrier so I got right to the point.

As we munched away on the complimentary chips and salsa, I gave them the scoop in its entirety. My family has never once questioned my career choices. I did get a little resistance when I chose work over college, but other than that I have enjoyed complete and total support from both of them. Part of this, I'm sure, comes from the fact that I have

79

only really ever wanted to do one thing with my life and have never strayed from that goal. I love my parents so much for being this way and I strive to be the same kind of backbone for my own kids.

Backstage at a speaking event with Mom and Dad, the two most supportive and loving parents a guy could ask for. 2009.

In addition to being a worrier, my mom is a crier. With tears streaming down her cheeks, she asked about my timeframe. I told her I was expected in Los Angeles within three weeks. E! was handling my move so all I was responsible for was finding a place to live once I got out there. When they saw that everything was in place, they congratulated me and we raised our glasses in a toast. Three Diet Cokes clinging in perfect harmony.

Speaking to my folks was easier than I had anticipated. I was expecting more tears and more questions. Informing the radio station, however, would require some smooth talkin' and some tap dancin'. I had three months left on my contract and, if they wanted to be sticklers about it, they could have made things difficult for me. The timing wasn't the best, either. Kenny Knight, our high profile afternoon jock, had just announced that he was leaving to do a morning show in Philadelphia. This meant that the station would be losing two of its key players. I walked in to the General Manager's office knowing that if push came to shove I would personally buy out my own contract. Nothing was going to stand in my way of getting to Hollywood.

Our GM, Bill Viands, was a soft spoken man but he also believed in towing the company line. He listened intently as I told him of my intentions and agreed that it was not something I could afford to pass up. People in the entertainment industry are all too aware of the fact that big breaks don't come along that often. He expressed that the station would hate to see me go but wished me the best. I was so relieved. As we shook hands, I made sure to let him know how much I appreciated everything the station had done for me. I believe in giving credit where credit is due. None of us get anywhere alone. Bill took some risks on me and invested a lot of the station's budget into promoting my show. I was grateful and I wanted him to know it. Were it not for the doors that opened because of my radio show and all of the Rick Idol hoopla, E! would have still been nothing more to me than a cable channel that I flipped on at bedtime.

Nikki and I had been together for two years and, by this point, were barely holding it together. The amount of time we spent with each other had decreased significantly and, though I still cared for her, I had begun dating another girl named Stephanie. Nikki knew we were growing apart and threw herself into her final year at college and into her music as a distraction. We never spoke of anything of substance and were no longer involving the other in our lives.

I don't mind breakups if they are handled properly. Most of us realize that relationships usually end. Those that last forever are extremely rare and I question just how happy the couple *really* is after, say, sixty years. Like many couples, Nikki and I had become more of a habit. I have two regrets when it comes to Nikki. The first is that I wasn't empathetic enough when I told her I was moving to L.A.. I presented it in a "this is how it is now deal with it" kind of way and that's not how I really felt. I knew I would miss her and I knew she would be sad. I wish I had been more compassionate. I also regret what occurred a few days after Nikki and I had decided to go our separate ways.

Stephanie had been my date for my farewell broadcast at Stagez. It was a great night and Milan, in typical fashion, pulled out all the stops. The thousands of people who showed up enjoyed free food, an open bar, and live bands until the early morning hours. It was a blast. When the party was over, Stephanie and I went back to my place. She was an extremely sexy woman. Long blonde hair, blue eyes, fantastic dresser, and a sharp wit. Spending the night with Stephanie was never a dull experience.

My phone rang early the next morning. With Stephanie's sleepy head resting heavily on my chest, I struggled to reach over and hit the speaker button. It was my mother calling to see how the party was. Steph decided she would have a little fun trying to get me to lose my composure while speaking to my mom.

81

I was doing a fine job of holding it together when I heard a noise that made me freeze. Someone was putting a key in my front door. I told Stephanie to stop messing around so I could listen more closely. Sure enough, I heard the unmistakable sound of my front door opening and closing. Stephanie and I just looked at each other. It took Nikki all of about five seconds to walk from the living room to the bedroom.

She had come only to return my apartment key, but ended up getting the shock of a lifetime. There, naked as the day we were born, were the man Nikki was trying desperately to hold onto and the girl who was keeping that from happening. I have no idea how long the three of us just stared at one another. All I can recall is that the silence was broken by the voice of my mother...still on speakerphone..."T? Are you still there?"

I kicked into damage control mode and disconnected the phone from midair as I jumped out of bed. Crying and yelling hysterically, Nikki ran into the living room. I followed her and tried to speak calmly but there was no diffusing the situation. She had seen more than she had ever wanted to see and nothing I was going to say or do would erase that image from her mind.

It was killing me to see her so hurt. I knew we couldn't be together but this was not how I wanted it to end. I would never wish that kind of pain on anyone, especially Nikki. I told her we could talk about this later but it would probably be best if she left. I picked up her purse and handed it to her.

"This isn't even my purse, you asshole!"

Why every young woman had to use a tiny black backpack as a purse back then is beyond me. It certainly didn't help the situation any. How Nikki could tell her's from Stephanie's remains a mystery, but the fact remains I had rubbed salt in the wound by handing her the wrong bag. This was the trigger that turned her sadness into anger and she stormed out.

I walked back to the bedroom, crawled into bed and pulled the covers over my head. Stephanie, ever the sarcastic one, said she knew of a way to take my mind off of what had just happened. I told her I was far from being in the mood for that, even though we were both still completely nude.

"I'm not talking about that, silly. I'm talking about pancakes."

Pancakes do make *everything* better.

*Hosting E!'s coverage of the
2007 Academy Awards in Hollywood.*

When I began working at E!, the network was still in its relative infancy. In the mid 90's nearly everything was produced in house so everyone worked together to put out the best shows possible. In addition to *Coming Attractions*, I hosted *Talk Soup*, *E! News Daily*, *Wild On*, and countless red carpet events. I was able to travel and interview the biggest stars in the world. Even more important to me than all of that is the fact that E! allowed me to try new things when it came to developing my hosting style. Some of those things worked and some didn't. It was total trial and error, but even when I fell flat on my face, cracked a joke that didn't fly, or flubbed a line during a live show, no one ever belittled me for it. A more creative and encouraging environment one would be hard pressed to find. I enjoyed twelve amazing years on that network, met the woman who gave me my children, developed a million great relationships, and had a hell of a good time. But, truth be told, game shows are, and always will be, what tickle my professional fancy.

In the summer of 1999, I was in Spain shooting an episode of *Wild On!* for E!. Many people believe that show was all bikinis and bars but nothing could be further from the truth. What you saw on television is not at all what Brooke Burke, Jules Asner, Art Mann, myself, or any of the other hosts experienced while on location. The majority of that show was put together using b-roll camera footage. What we did as hosts was actually far less glamorous. Don't get me wrong, I enjoyed circling the globe and visiting places I normally would never have gone, but the travel became exhausting and the content of the show left quite a bit to be desired.

On the final leg of our trip to Spain, my crew and I traveled from Barcelona to Valencia to cover what the locals call La Tomatina.

Originated in 1945, La Tomatina is nothing more than a large, messy tomato fight. On the last Wednesday of every August, thousands of young men and women gather in the center of town and await the arrival of trucks filled with 150,000 tomatoes. As the plump, ripe pieces of fruit are dumped into the street and squashed in order to prevent serious injury, the soon to be warriors begin singing, chanting, and working themselves up into a frenzy.

Finally, a shot is fired to signal the beginning of the fight. For one hour, we hurled tomatoes at complete strangers. My cameraman and I were walking targets as I tried to record a blow by blow account of what was happening. Each time the camera would come on I would take a tomato blast in the face. All around us people were slipping and sliding on the red, juicy streets. Some sought refuge in doorways and alleys only to be discovered and bombarded.

A second gun shot sounded to signify the end of the battle. FIre trucks made their way through the narrow, cobblestone streets and sprayed us all down with their giant hoses. It was a fun, yet frightful, experience. Some suffered minor injuries, but most relished in the post fight adrenaline as they sloshed back to wherever they had come from.

There was a message waiting for me when I returned to my hotel. Nicole had called me from Los Angeles and said it was important. It is apparently customary for the locals to tear off the t-shirts worn by others after La Tomatina so, shirtless and exhausted, I carried my weary bones up to my room, dug my international calling card out of my wallet, and dialed the United States.

Nicole laughed hysterically as I relayed the day's events. Reliving the experience made me appreciate just how unique of a day it had really been. The reason for Nicole's call was to inform me of an audition that she thought I should make every effort to attend. Though I had planned on staying in Spain for a couple of days after we wrapped the episode, she said this show was a great opportunity and one she would hate to see me miss.

"What kind of show is it?" I asked.

"It's a pop culture trivia show called *Hollywood Showdown*," she replied. "The producer, Sande Stewart, is a game show legend and it looks as if Game Show Network has already committed to 65 episodes. I really think you should change your ticket and come back for this."

For Nicole to suggest that I leave beautiful Spain early meant that this had the potential to be something big. I called the airline, swallowed the change fee, and headed back to America.

My first meeting with Sande Stewart was love and respect at first sight. Sande is known for having a rough exterior but he is honestly one of the most generous and intelligent men I've ever met. From day one, he took me under his wing and has, over the years, molded me into everything a game show host should be.

I was fortunate enough to be selected as the host of *Hollywood Showdown* and, along with announcer Randy West, producer Cathy Dawson, and the rest of our stellar crew, went on to enjoy 130 episodes on Game Show Network and years worth of reruns on TV Guide Channel.

Unlike other projects I had been involved with up to that point, *Hollywood Showdown* was more than just a gig. I knew the moment I set foot on that stage and the cameras starting rolling that I was meant to be a game show host. There is nothing more rewarding than sharing a life changing moment with a contestant. If you tally up all of the cash and prizes I have awarded to contestants over the years on *Showdown*, *Whammy!*, *Instant Millionaire*, *Family Game Night*, and across the country with *The Price Is Right Live!*, the total comes to over $28,000,000. That number includes new cars that allow people to get to work or seek employment. It includes money that has been used to get families out of debt, purchase a new home, or put children through college. It includes prizes like much needed refrigerators to keep food fresh and televisions so families can stay in and enjoy a movie together.

As your host, I see things that you can't see at home. I notice the quivering of a contestant's lip and the beads of sweat forming on the brow as they decide whether to stop with what they've already won or go for the grand prize. I hear what family members say to one another as they rush the stage after a million dollar win. I cherish these moments and will never tire of them.

The game show genre continues to graciously accept me as one of it's own. I've been honored with a Daytime Emmy in the Outstanding Game Show Host category for my work on *Family Game Night*. In addition to Sande, I've been mentored by Bob Barker and stood alongside the great Peter Tomarken on the *Whammy!* set. I've hosted over 1,000 performances of *The Price Is Right Live!* stage show and continuously have the chance to meet fellow game show fans across the country. It is certainly true that E! Entertainment Television will always be a second home to me, but game shows are where I will always hang my hat.

Pinpointing the one moment or person that constitutes my "big break" would be an impossible task. Maybe it was the Rick Idol era. Perhaps it was walking over to MTV with my demo tape or Curt Sharp's generosity. Some may say it was Nicole Taylor's willingness to sign me or Dan Gibson choosing me over the other candidates for *Coming Attractions*. Maybe it was Sande Stewart seeing me at that first *Hollywood Showdown* audition and recognizing the next incarnation of the game show host.

Personally, I say it's all of the above. There is no such thing as an overnight success. That is precisely why I called this book my *road* to success and fulfillment rather than a *guide*. As much as we'd like for there to be a magic pill that can instantly turn you into a rock star, a great parent, a CEO, or Hall of Fame athlete, it just doesn't exist. But look around and what you *will* find are opportunities.

In this day and age you have the world at your fingertips with the internet. You can learn everything about anything at anytime simply by pressing the right buttons on your keyboard. We have the ability to download books and videos that allow us to advance in our chosen fields. You can attend college in your pajamas and you can correspond with people on the other side of the planet while sitting at your kitchen table. The opportunities are endless and the only thing holding you back from reaching your goals is *you*.

You are a living, breathing success story. Somewhere someone is looking up to you right at this very moment. You are unique and possess so much more than what you are aware of. People enjoy seeing others succeed and there is no greater feeling than being a part of someone else's victory. Generosity and peace are the norm when it comes to human nature. I encourage you now to pursue what you have been dreaming of with this final thought in mind...

It doesn't matter who you know,
when you know who you are.

CHAPTER 6
MY GRAND PRIZES

Daddy how does thing fly? And a hundred other where's and why's. I really don't know but I try. Thank God for kids.
-Oak Ridge Boys

IT HITS YOU OUT of nowhere. It comes upon you so suddenly, like that poor guy at the ball game who looks down to grab his beer and looks back up just in time to get cranked in the kisser by a foul ball. The urge to have children is almost as instantaneous but the life changing effects of becoming a parent are far more enjoyable than those that come from being knocked unconscious at Fenway Park.

I don't think Silver and I ever really laid out exactly when we wanted to start a family. There was no question children were in the cards, but the decision of when that would happen for us was left in Mother Nature's hands. As it turns out, everything kicked into high gear one evening after dinner and margaritas at our favorite Mexican restaurant in Marina del Rey, CA. There must have been something special in the tequila, or maybe it was just the ocean air, but that night at the beach was a life changer.

I remember the day Silver told me she was pregnant. I called home from the set of E! and could hear something different in the sound of her voice. It wasn't frustration for leaving the toilet seat up or curiosity caused by the rattling in the air conditioner. It was something I'd never heard before. I've never been the type to "talk about this later" so I pressed her until she finally spilled the wonderful news.

Just as every young girl waits for the day when the man of her dream asks her to marry him, or when a game show contestant finally hears the words, "A brand, new car!" such is the thrill I felt when she told me were going to have a baby. It was complete and overwhelming elation in the purest form and I rushed home to be with her. Traffic in LA is never cooperative, but this day seemed more congested than usual as I crept along the 101 at a snail's pace. I flew through the door and took her in my arms as we celebrated what was, at that very moment, only a tiny embryo seeking nourishment seeking inside of her. From that day on, life had new meaning for me.

At the time, we were living in what we called "The Treehouse." It was a 70's style apartment in the Studio City hills across from Jerry's

Deli. It was pretty evident that we enjoyed the close proximity to Jerry's because I'd put on about ten pounds as a result of the brick sized pieces of carrot cake we enjoyed a few nights a week.

We loved our funky little retreat but the seventy steps leading up to the front door soon became a bit of a strain for the mommy-to-be. We decided to pack our belongings and head back out to the beach. I knew the fresh, ocean air would be good for both her and the baby. And getting away from the carrot cake at Jerry's would be good for me. We rented a huge apartment on Voyage Street in Marina del Rey. The landlady was a Persian woman who could not of been nicer when we signed the lease and agreed to pay her $3,400 a month. Boy, would that soon change.

I started to get busier and busier as the months began to pass. *Whammy!* was in its second season, I was still doing the occasional live event for E!, and I had just signed on to co-host a movie review show with Leonard Maltin called *Hot Ticket*. We were doing well financially, hitting all of our doctor's appointments, and counting the seconds until we could find out if we were having a boy or a girl.

Many people choose not to find out the sex of their child because they want it to be a surprise. How much of a surprise can it be? It's either heads or tales, right? We wanted to know because we wanted to begin to give him/her an identity. I wanted to talk to my child and not have it be the generic baby gibberish. We wanted to start thinking of names, decorating the nursery, buying clothes. We wanted it all.

Each time Silver had an ultrasound I would hold my breath until the technician would tell us everything was in order. I'd be a nervous wreck but she was always cool. On the day of the big reveal, the tech made the obligatory "well endowed" jokes that I am sure she had made to thousands of couples before and, like thousands of couples before, we responded with the obligatory chuckle. She announced that we would be having a son. I'd had no preference before the announcement, but I was elated by the news. My boy, little Newton, now seemed to be one giant step closer.

Silver was almost eight months pregnant when I was invited to co-host the Miss Universe pageant with Elle McPherson and Naomi Campbell in San Juan, Puerto Rico. Although this would be the biggest television audience I had ever been in front of, my first reaction was to pass on it. We were too close to her due date and there was no way I was going to be away from her. Silver insisted that I accept the offer. She felt it was an opportunity that was too good to pass up but I refused to go unless she could come with me. Since it would be a quick trip, her doctor gave us the local hospital info and the go ahead. Though still not completely convinced it was the right thing to do, I went ahead and signed the contract. We were packing for the trip a couple of days later when there was a knock on our door.

Ernie was our neighbor. A nice guy in his fifties who was an attorney by trade but made a substantial amount of money on the side by counting cards at blackjack in casinos around the world. Ernie had some news to share with us. Apparently he'd had his apartment inspected and found large amounts of the mold called Stachybotrys in the walls. I couldn't believe what I was hearing. Why now? Why us? Here I had moved my wife and unborn child out to the beach and was paying an obscene amount in rent every month only to throw them right into a pit of toxic fungus. And I find all of this out the day before we were to leave for the biggest show of my career.

I needed someone, anyone, to tell me this was not what it appeared to be. My repeated attempts to reach our landlady were unsuccessful. The phone would ring continuously until I finally had no other choice but to leave her a voicemail. She was clearly avoiding my calls and that only made my suspicions worse.

The next day, as we headed for LAX, my mind was on everything but Miss Universe. I was scared to death and the inflight entertainment certainly didn't help matters. They showed an episode of *48 Hours* that featured a piece on, you guessed it, mold.

The segment told the horrifying story of a family who had unknowingly been living with mold for years. As a result, the children had suffered long term physical and mental defects. I was trapped on that plane, unable to do anything, and about to jump out of my skin. Silver did her best to console me and assured me we would handle it all when we got back home. We landed in Puerto Rico, checked into our suite, and tried to let the beautiful island breeze blow all of the negativity away.

With everything that was on my mind at the time...the baby on the way, the live broadcast around the word, the mold, I have to say I have seen few things more beautiful than my wife and her extended tummy laying out by the pool in San Juan with a bevy of Miss Universe contestants flocked around her. She was the center of attention as they asked her questions about the pregnancy and rubbed her belly. Even Donald Trump stopped to tell her how beautiful she looked.

I phoned the landlady repeatedly from Puerto Rico and finally, after two days and almost a hundred dollars in long distance charges, got to speak to her. She assured me there was no mold and that I had absolutely nothing to worry about. Although I knew there must be something amiss, her words provided enough relief to get me through the rest of the trip. The building, she said, had been thoroughly inspected when she purchased it a few years earlier and passed with flying colors. Ernie the attorney, however, had been doing his own research and discovered information to the contrary.

When we returned home, I was informed that our landlady had actually sued the previous owner for undisclosed water damage. She took the money from the lawsuit and, instead of making the necessary repairs, decided instead to just do a cover job. She lied and, by doing so, had put my family in danger. I hadn't even been married a year and my baby was still a fetus, but she was going to learn that you do not mess with the den when Papa Bear's around.

Thanks to all of the shows I had on the air at the time, money wasn't much of an issue. I immediately called independent inspectors out to the beach. Silver and I examined every nook and cranny of the place ourselves and discovered a patch of mold hiding behind our big screen television in the living room. We knew we had enough evidence for a strong case. This was further solidified one afternoon when I saw a few men lingering outside the building. I went out and introduced myself and came to discover they were insurance inspectors who had been called out by Ernie's attorneys. They were more than happy to look at my place and I was more than happy to let them in. It gave me all the confirmation I needed and also saved me the $5,000 that hiring my own inspectors would've cost.

Silver and I knew the most important thing facing us was finding a new place to live. We came across a cute little house in Bel Air at the top of Mulholland. As much as we hated saying goodbye to the beach, we packed up and headed for the hills. As the movers unpacked our belongings, I called my attorney, filled him in on the situation, and put the wheels of my first lawsuit into motion. My instructions to him were simple...show her no mercy.

Our landlord became an absolute nightmare. In response to my filing a lawsuit, she countersued on the grounds that I had broken my lease and claimed I now owed her thousands of dollars. Though a laughable reaction, at the time it only added stress and fuel to the fire. What should have been an easy fix between two adults became a complete waste of the taxpayers' money. She refused to show up for the first two depositions and then, at the third, pretended her English was too poor to understand anything that was being said. We were presented with one delay after another. All the while, Silver's belly continued to grow.

Finally, we reached a settlement which covered little more that my moving expenses. I had initially hoped there might be a little more coming our way, but by the time it was over I was just happy to put the whole mess behind me and focus on getting ready for our baby. The doctor's visits were making us both more and more excited to be parents. It was pretty obvious he was going to be a big boy and all we could think about was welcoming him into the world.

I've had many memorable conversations with many fascinating people in my life, but talking to your spouse about what name you want to give your child tops the list. This is their initial identity. It's what you, and everyone in the world, will refer to them as. It seems so important, and I guess it is, but I also feel that whatever name you give them becomes secondary to the people they become. We could have named our son Ozone and today we'd be saying "I can't imagine him being anything *but* an Ozone."

His name, we decided, would be Mason. Silver was raised in a little town in Virginia called Mason Neck. She'd never say it, but like most little girls I think she'd probably always had her future children's names picked out. To me it sounded strong and proud. It went well with Newton. It just struck me as *his* name.

Around mid June of 2001, Silver's doctor started to suggest we consider inducing labor if Mase didn't pop out on his own in the next week or two. If the fruit is ready to be picked then nothing good can come from leaving it on the tree. Made sense, I guess. We agreed and she contacted Cedars Sinai to schedule the arrival of our child.

It made me think about what the frontier days must have been like when women gave birth in a field or the stories I'd heard about women delivering in the back of taxis during rush hour. Here we were basically making an appointment to become parents in Beverly Hills. My ex sister in law gave birth to all three of her children in her bathtub at home. There is definitely something intimate and "hippy cool" about that, but when it came right down to it, we chose to trust modern medicine and let all of those health insurance premiums go to to work for us.

We were to arrive at the hospital at 6am on July 2 and Mason would arrive shortly thereafter.

You would think the night before a baby's arrival would be hectic and scattered. In reality, it was actually quite calm. I don't think it was because Silver and I were keeping our wits about us, instead I think it was because we were saying to ourselves, *"Oh my God! We're having a baby tomorrow."*

I can't speak as to what was going through Silver's mind. She gets quiet when the heat is on and this is how she functions best. Personally, I was barely able to contain my excitement. Even our dog, Congo, was staring at me as if I'd lost my mind.

Many people have the luxury of being surrounded by their loved ones almost daily. I do not. My parents had flown in from the midwest. To have my folks, my wife, and a child all under one roof the very next day was going to be a real treasure for me.

I was already so in love with Mason. Just his image on the ultrasound, hearing the thump of his heartbeat in the doctor's stethoscope, and feeling him kick when I placed my hand on Silver's stomach was enough to lock me in the palm of this boy's hand for a lifetime. The fact that my son was hours away was beyond my wildest comprehension. It was like trying to fall asleep underneath a cloud that was sprinkling drops of love, anxiety, fear, excitement, joy, and the unknown down upon you.

Silver had no problem falling asleep. I, however, was tossing and turning and had only been asleep an hour or two when the phone rang. A ringing telephone at 1a.m. will startle anyone on any given night but it nearly threw me out of bed on this particular evening. I was on high alert as it was. It was the hospital calling to say they were full and needed to push back our arrival time.

Now, when such preparation and anticipation goes into an event as important as *giving birth*, you can't postpone it on such short notice. You can reschedule a business meeting or even a date with a supermodel if you absolutely must, but not the arrival of Mason. He was ready to come out and we were ready for him.

I had been told by a friend who's wife had delivered at Cedars that the nurses there were not impressed by show business folks at all. I rarely pull the "I'm on TV" card, but was certainly willing to in this case if it meant Silver would have the red carpet rolled out for her. We ignored the postponement and arrived at our originally scheduled time. Turns out the nurses who were there for the birth of Michael Jackson's kids weren't that impressed with the guy from basic cable. I needed to resort to my Plan B. Gifts.

I have a deep respect for teachers and for nurses. Both put up with a level of BS that none of us are equipped to handle. Nurses work incredibly long hours and deal with stressful situations on a constant basis. They accept crisis as the norm so I thought it might be nice (and serve as an attention grabber) if I brought them a large assortment of brownies to nibble on while they took care of all the crazed parents and screaming babies in the maternity ward.

Turns out it worked perfectly! Our main nurse gave us a big, beautiful smile when I presented her with my platter of schmooze. There was no misunderstanding as to what these desserts represented. We wanted the best treatment possible. Looking back I'm sure we would have been treated just as well without bringing goodies, but it seemed like a good strategy at the time.

My parents dropped us off at the Emergency entrance and Silver was immediately placed into a wheelchair and rolled away to our private room. As I filled out the necessary paperwork, I had a surreal realization. Two of us would enter, but three of us would leave. It was really starting to hit me.

The staff came in and out throughout the morning to give Silver all the standard tests. Around lunchtime, we began to induce labor by administering Potocin, a drug which slowly stimulates contractions.

It is at this point where I salute Silver. As a matter of fact, I bow before her. Though she never showed it, she must have been scared senseless. Throughout her entire pregnancy Silver was devoted to Mason's health. She was the same way with Kiki. A healthy diet, exercise, no alcohol, and consistent monitoring by her doctor. She never cut corners when it came to the well being of our children and she still doesn't. As a man and a father there is nothing more I could ask for. I am eternally grateful for all she has done for our babies.

I know many women who take a much more casual approach to having kids. They schedule a C Section, load up on the epidural, and the next thing you know their nanny suddenly has her hands full. Nothing wrong with that. To each her own, but that was not Silver. She read everything she could get her hands on and had this whole childbirth thing by the horns. She even chose to go with only a walking epidural. I was not only proud, I was in awe. She was about to pass a bowling ball through a garden hose and was doing it, for the most part, au natural.

Her contractions began to get stronger and stronger as the day progressed. The more her body prepared to give birth to our precious son the more her mind focused on the process. I would periodically run out to the waiting room and give my parents an update. I was wearing a Missouri Baptist College t-shirt, the school where my Nana worked for so many years, as a way of having her there with me on this monumental day.

Eventually Silver's doctor started popping in which let us know that the time was drawing near. By late afternoon the energy in the room had shifted and a baby we would soon be holding.

Silver was breathing and focusing. In that situation, the best thing the father can do is stand close by and let her know you're there for whatever she needs. I didn't want to crowd her or smother her. This was her body and no one knew what was happening better than she did.

After a few pushing sessions, the doctor decided it was time to enter the home stretch. I was asked to turn the video camera off for legal reasons which was a bit of a disappointment but not one I was willing to dispute. I took my position just to Silver's left and let these two women do their thing.

Silver huffed, puffed, and pushed. The doctor and I offered encouragement but she didn't need it. She was in charge. She huffed, puffed, and pushed some more. Soon the doctor looked up at me from between my wife's legs and smiled. She signaled me over to take a look. When I did, I saw the top of my son's head. It was covered in dark hair which the doc twirled in her fingers. It was so unbelievably beautiful.

More huffing. More puffing. More pushing, until...we heard his cry. Mason Todd Newton entered the world at 7:39pm on July 2, 2001. There are no words to describe the love we both had for him the moment we saw him. Only a parent can truly know what that emotion, one that far surpasses any word, feels like. Mason, as you read this, it was the most powerful and meaningful moment either of us had ever experienced.

We had asked in advance for some time alone with our baby. The staff, after making sure Mommy and baby were healthy, obliged.

I encourage every new set of parents to request some alone time. Life becomes so hectic when a baby arrives that these first few moments are something you will undoubtedly cherish forever.

The door closed behind them and suddenly it was just the three of us. I watched Silver as she held Mason on her chest. She is a beautiful woman, but she had never been more radiant than she was the first time she held our babies. I'll never forget watching her smile as she told Mason how perfect he was and played with the dimple in his chin.

For nine months these two had been one. She had brought this child to life and now he was in her arms. I can only imagine what that must have felt like. Fathers don't get to experience that, but mothers deserve to have a moment that belongs exclusively to them for all they sacrifice. I took picture after picture but they don't do the moments justice. It's the type of thing that you can only enjoy and appreciate as it is happening.

The nurse returned and said we needed to give the baby his first bath. By this point I had run out to the waiting room, thrown my arms in the air and screamed "He's here!" to my parents.

The new grandparents met us at the nursery and watched through the glass as the nurse bathed my little boy and put him in his first diaper. Never out of our sight while in the hospital, I wheeled him back to Silver's room. By looking at her it was hard to believe she had just delivered a baby. A true warrior. I asked her if there was anything she wanted. "A Pepsi," is all she said.

A few years later we decided it was time for baby number two. I was on the road hosting *The Price Is Right Live!* at the time and we were performing mainly in Kansas City. Whenever I travel I always come home on my off days to be with the kids. I did when I was married and I hold to it still today. I only travel to support my family and want every free moment to be spent at home.

These particular trips back to L.A. had a purpose, though. In addition to seeing my son, who was three at the time, I was doing my husbandly duty and attempting to impregnate my lovely bride. Duty may not be the right word, but you get my point.

Silver's doctor suggested that, due to my travel schedule, we consider storing some of my love juice so it would be accessible when Silver was ovulating regardless if I was home or not. Not exactly my definition of romantic, but it's common practice with families who are in the same boat we were. We thought it couldn't hurt.

Banking sperm requires two things of a man: strong focus and the ability to temporarily set aside your pride. I showed up at the office in Encino, was handed a small cup, and led into a private room. I cracked a few jokes out of sheer embarrassment, but they were completely lost on the nurse who had clearly ushered countless men through this process. My only instructions were to make sure I ejaculated directly into the cup and wash my hands when I was finished. I'm not sure these notes were needed as this was far from being my first rodeo, but I nodded affirmatively as the nurse closed the door.

The clinic was kind enough to provide some magazines and VHS tapes for my pleasure and stimulation. They were a little outdated and not really of the genre I prefer, so I chose to close my eyes and use my own material. Whatever my lustfully creative mind came up with that day seemed to do the job. I stood, screwed the lid tightly on the cup, and paraded down to the front desk. Deposit complete...and not a bad way to start the day, I might add.

As it turns out, the whole adventure was unnecessary. Silver became pregnant with our second child the old fashioned way. Again, I was elated. We had a better idea of what was ahead this time and, to make it even more special, Mason was around to watch his little brother or sister grow in his mommy's belly.

By this time we had left the little Bel Air house and purchased our first home in Tarzana. It was in a cute little neighborhood with lots of charm and families around our age. We were living the American dream. A house, two cars, two kids...the whole enchilada.

As Silver's pregnancy progressed, I began taking less work on the road. It was difficult being away from Mason and I wanted to be present for Silver's doctor's appointments. I also wanted to spend as much time at the new house as possible. I was enjoying family life and wanted to soak up as much of it as I could.

As with Mason, we decided we wanted to know the sex of the baby and, again, I had no preference as to which side of the coin came up in the toss. Heads-I have two sons. Tails-one of each.

At the ultrasound appointment the coin was flipped and tails it was. We were having a baby girl. Nothing in the world prepares a man for that. In an instant, her whole life zoomed through my mind. Her birth, losing her first tooth, her first date, her first heartbreak, learning to drive a car, her having a baby...all of it. I know now that it was my way of acknowledging to myself that I would always be there for her no matter what she needed. She would forever be my little angel.

In addition to all of the previously mentioned benefits, knowing the sex of your child in advance allows you to spend even more money on clothes that you know the child will outgrow within weeks. Everything pink, yellow, light blue, and any shade of purple came home with us. Teddy bears, rainbows, you name it! My baby was a little fashionista and she wasn't even here yet.

Silver was enjoying another perfect pregnancy. Believe me, I know how fortunate we are for that. Part of it was due to Silver being a healthy person, of course, but when it comes to pregnancy most of it is out of your hands. We're so lucky to live in a country where we can enjoy all of the benefits of modern medicine to regulate the baby's development the whole way. When our doctor told us our little girl was ready to come out, we made an appointment with the hospital to welcome a new baby Newton into the world.

Since my parents were in town for the birth of Mason, we decided to invite Silver's mom in for the arrival of our daughter. She was planning on staying for a week or two after to help out around the house. Things were a little different for us this time because of Mason. He was just as excited to meet his baby sister as we were. At the time, we had a wonderful nanny that he adored working for us a few days a week and she would there, as well.

At the last minute, Silver's mother's plans changed and she was no longer able to come to California for the birth. I was pretty upset by it because I couldn't understand why anyone would want to miss such an event, but it was out of my control. What upset me the most was my parents had stepped aside on this one and now would unnecessarily miss the birth of what will most likely be their last grandchild.

On March 10, 2005, Silver and I drove to Tarzana Medical Center to have our baby. Joanna, our nanny, stayed with Mason. It's strange how you feel like such a pro the second time around. Were we nervous? You bet. But we had some idea of what was in store and were better able to roll with the punches.

Tarzana Medical was a little more intimate and not quite as overwhelming as Cedars was. I mentioned how brave Silver was with Mason, but she blew my mind this time when she told the nurse that she didn't want any epidural at all for the delivery. She was going all frontier on us and was willing to take the pain if it meant not having any foreign chemicals put into her system. I have a high tolerance of pain. Never had a painkiller in my life. But this was going above and beyond.

Kingsley (Kiki) Faith Newton came to us that day at 1:21pm. A whole new kind of love filled my heart as I watched my baby daughter being born. She was everything that is beautiful. She was my little girl. I call her Cupcake because when I kissed her that very first time her little forehead smelled like a warm baked good. Delicious!

I spent the remainder of the day with Silver and Kingsley then went home that evening to be with Mason. He was only 3 and I knew he had to be wondering what was going on. I didn't want him to wait any longer than he had to.

That night was the first night he had ever slept away from his mother so we made it a special guy's night by watching *Thomas the Tank Engine* in bed until we fell asleep.

The next morning, he and I woke up early and went to the hospital to see the baby. Just like that, we were four.

Mason and Kiki. The loves of my life.

My parents always said that children grow up too fast. That couldn't be more true. One major reason for writing this book is so my kids will always have a written document of my love for them. I have a stack of journals that I have been writing in since we found out Silver was pregnant with Mason. The pages are filled with things we did, things they said, what I was feeling, and words I wanted to say to them that they were perhaps too young to understand at the time. This book fulfills a similar purpose.

Mason and Kiki, my life was not whole until you two came into it. Not even close. Other than a few special moments, I really can't recall what things were like before you.

Believe me, I never intended to be a father who travels as much as I do. I wish I could be there to tuck you guys in every night and make you pancakes every morning. I don't even know how to make pancakes, but I would learn to make the best pancakes that ever swam in syrup if given the opportunity.

I hope, when you have kids of your own, you don't find yourself trotting from city to city in order to care for them. I love what I do, but being away from your family is the most difficult kind of loneliness.

I guess in some ways I'm luckier than a lot of dads out there. I know men who leave for the office before their kids wake up and don't get home until after bedtime. I wouldn't want that. I'm fortunate in that my schedule allows for me to always be home for birthdays, Christmas, big school events, etc. But I'm admittedly a greedy man and would much prefer to have it all.

I'll often meet men after a speech who are aware of my traveling and ask how I manage it. I tell them exactly what former Vice President Al Gore told me one night in Nashville.

I had just finished a New Year's Eve show in Orlando and hopped on a plane to Nashville. Mr. Gore and his foundation,The Climate Project, had graciously selected me to be one of 1,000 people around the world authorized to give his award winning *"An Inconvenient Truth"* presentation.

He and Tipper took a few of us out for dinner one evening as a break from all the science, slides, and global warming talk. Like me, Gore is a "family first" man and I knew that if anyone could enlighten me on how to balance work and home efficiently it would be him. I followed him as he excused himself from the table to go get a drink at the bar.

Mr. Gore is a class act. He looks you in the eye when he speaks and you really feel as if he listens to every word you say. One can't help but think he gets a little of this from spending so much time with Clinton. Political osmosis, if you will.

Taking advantage of our moment alone, I told him that my career was beginning to pull me away from home more and more and I didn't see things changing anytime soon. Mr. Gore nodded his head and gave me a little smile that showed he understood exactly where I was coming from. It was genuine. Politicians are the best schmoozers on the planet but game show hosts run a close second so I can detect a lack of sincerity when one presents itself. This was the real thing.

Al Gore is constantly bombarded with fans, climate junkies, and people wanting to pitch business deals and I believe he found my situation to be a refreshing change. I told him that my kids were young and how I hated missing even a single moment with them. I expressed my fear that the need to earn a living might pull me away from important milestones that I'll never get a second chance of sharing. I expressed the confusion, for lack of a better term, of my true responsibility as a father. Do I spend every night at home knowing that I am not living up to my full potential as a provider, or do I seek out every professional opportunity in order to give them the best life possible? As smooth as a game show host holding a card with the answer to a million dollar question, the former VP of the United States of America...the man who, in my opinion, *should* have been President, gave me advice worth more to me than gold. If you are a father struggling with the same issue, I now gladly pass it on to you.

Meeting Al Gore days before he won the Oscar for
An Inconvenient Truth. 2007.

Al Gore explained that he always...I repeat,*always*...keeps a handwritten date book. I know it's old school. Electronic calendars are now standard on any smart phone or computer, and no one is more connected to modern computer technology than Al Gore, but he has always maintained a written itinerary. When an appointment was scheduled he'd write it down in pencil. When a family obligation or a "do not miss" event came up he would enter it in pen. Events that were written in pen never, for any reason, got cancelled or rescheduled. This is the ultimate example of prioritization. It requires a great deal of self discipline, but the results are tried and true. I've worked with countless men who are desperately in search of that balance between work and family. I now had the answer. Family first. No matter what.

I'm sure many will read this and say, "Todd that's a lot easier said than done." They're right. In today's world we compete harder than our fathers before us had to in order to bring home the bacon.

With cell phones, unlimited calling plans, and Skype it's much easier to stay connected when work pulls you away. The days of working 9-5 are nearly extinct and men and women are literally going to the far ends of the Earth in order to earn a living.

Much of my traveling I bring upon myself as I choose to fly myself home on every off day regardless of how much the ticket may cost or how little time I may be able to spend. Those moments with Mason and Kiki recharge, reenergize, and revitalize my soul and allow me to keep going.

I absolutely love what I do for a living and everything that comes with it. Even the crazy travel schedule. I don't work so hard because I love earning upgrades on every major airline. I do it so that my children can play sports and take horseback riding lessons. I do it so that we can go see movies, have fun dinners, and enjoy the finer things in life. Most importantly, I do it so that they will have every available opportunity to go to college and pursue all of their dreams.

As I sit here in room 2906 of the beautiful Lowe's Hotel in Miami, FL, I see people laying out on the sand enjoying the south beach sun. My body is here, still wearing the suit I wore to speak for 800 people earlier today, but my heart is with my two kids who are sitting in their respective classrooms learning about science, math, and life. I know quite a bit about life. Not everything, of course, but enough to know that *they* are what it's all about.

Champ and Cupcake-wherever you may go and whatever you may do...I will always be right here. I am so grateful for the opportunity to be your father. You make everyday unique and eventful. I am so proud of both of you, not only for who you are today, but also for who you will become tomorrow.

Let these words forever serve as a message of my deep and eternal love for the both of you. Please tuck it safely away in your hearts and carry it with you always.

-Dad

CHAPTER 7
ARE YOU THERE GOD?

Religions are necessarily splitting people, creating a duality in the human mind. That is their way of exploiting you. If you are whole, you are beyond their control. If you are cut in fragments, then all your strength is destroyed, all your power, your dignity abolished. If you are left just the way you are born-natural, without any interference from the so-called religious leaders, you will have freedom, independence, integrity. You cannot be enslaved.
-Osho

IF HEAVEN WERE TO have an answering machine, I imagine the outgoing message would consist of something along the lines of:

"Hello, you've reached Heaven. There's no one here to take your call. We're not out running errands or in the shower..THERE IS JUST NO ONE HERE! Sorry to disappoint you. Please seek other means of solving your problems."

Yes, I am an atheist. Thank God/Buddha/Allah/Oprah that we live in a country where I have the right to say that openly because, for so many, the word is borderline taboo. It does not mean that I worship the devil (there is no devil), nor does it mean that I look down on anyone else for their religious beliefs. It simply means that *I* do not believe in the idea of an omnipotent (all powerful), omniscient (all knowing), omnipresent (possessing the ability to be everywhere) bearded man in the sky. So, since I live my life as a non-believer, thus not believing in theism, I must identify myself as an a-theist.

Many people with whom I have had discussions on religion have felt the need to pad it by saying that perhaps I am merely agnostic. Agnostic, by definition, means that I believe that a higher power such as God cannot be proved or disproved. It implies that I loiter on the corner of Maybe St. and I Don't Know Blvd.

There is a vague grain of truth in the definition. It certainly has not been proven-not even close-that a god exists. And let us remember that the burden of truth lies with those who make the claim for Him, not with the non believers. But saying that I am agnostic is pretty much the same thing as going to the track and betting on every horse in the race to win. No matter how the pony runs you still get to cash in a ticket.

The Bible, though a fascinating collection of fables and contradictions (see Genesis 32:30 then 1 Timothy 6:16 as an example), is proof of nothing more than the fact that storytellers and leaders of two thousand years ago had a clear agenda. That agenda included maintaining order by instituting guilt and fear among the masses. If you tried to instill those beliefs today people would call your bluff before the end of your 20 second segment on CNN Headline News, yet a 2011 Gallup poll shows that 92% of individuals still believe in what was inaccurately depicted, exaggerated, and set forth all those centuries ago.

A man I have great respect for is fellow atheist and Las Vegas performer Penn Jillette of the famed magic duo *Penn & Teller.* In the years I have been working on the Vegas strip, I've had the opportunity to meet Penn on several occasions and have found him to be a man who speaks his mind in a very well thought out and respectful way. It is Penn's opinion, and mine as well, that you cannot truly be agnostic. You either live your life day to day believing there is a higher power or you don't. I don't. And guess what? Believing in a mythical, undocumented being who resides in a nonexistent utopia is not required for me, or for *YOU,* to be a good person!

It may come as a shock to many, but living each day with love, compassion, and respect for your fellow man and the planet on which we live is all you need. Karma, positive energy, and all of that other nonsense is just rhetoric created by people who need an excuse to do the right thing. I don't rescue animals from shelters because I hope it will lead to something nice happening to me down the line. I adopt these pets because they are precious animals who need a loving home and, when I am able, I provide one for them. Karma Shmarma, just do what your gut tells you is the right thing to do and you'll live a happy, fruitful existence. Believe me, your parents did not spend the first eighteen years of your life teaching you the difference between right and wrong just so they could hear themselves speak.

One thing I say in my *The Choice Is Yours* presentation is that you must learn to trust yourself. If you trust no one else in this world, trust who you are. The problem is not with those of us who choose not to look to the heavens for truth and salvation, but rather with those who have chosen to look nowhere *but* the heavens.

Every nonbeliever I have spoken with can recall the exact moment they had their revelation. Just as preachers and prophets stand on the pulpit and testify about the time God spoke directly to them and gave them their mission in life (and why they need your money to make it happen), we can remember when we knew it was more than likely untrue. For me, it was in late June of 2001.

I was born and raised in a nice, Baptist household. My mother still sings in the church choir and my dad ran the athletics department at our church. As a kid, I always found the fellow church goers friendly, but I despised going to Sunday School. Waking up early, putting on uncomfortable clothes, and rushing out the door to have people tell us stories and how to behave was never my idea of a good time. Who would hold any type of school on a Sunday, anyway? That concept alone is ridiculous. But, regardless of how I felt about it, we were still required to go to church each week.

Tradition has it that at the end of every long, drawn out, monotonous church service two things always happen. The first is they pass around an offering plate. Actually, several plates are passed around at once to make sure no good Christian's tithe is overlooked. The customary donation is ten percent of one's income. This money is handed directly over to the church (which pays no taxes) and then supposedly used for "fellowship" purposes.

The second consistency is what is referred to as "the invitation." This is where people from the congregation are invited down to the front of the auditorium to accept Jesus as their lord and savior. Much to the disappointment of the attendees, Jesus is never free to attend the services himself, but most preachers attempt to fill in for him by striking the arms-outstretched-on-the-cross pose in order to enhance the experience. Truth be told, this is much like catching a Broadway play and finding out the star is sick so you'll be enjoying the understudy in today's performance. It must work, though, because there is never a Sunday where people don't flock to the front of the stage to let Jesus into their hearts and have their sins washed away.

We are taught in Sunday School that this is one of the biggest decisions you'll make in your lifetime. Forget purchasing a home, enlisting in the military, choosing your spouse, voting, deciding when to have children, or selecting a form of birth control...this is *big*. Personally, I made this decision when I was seven years old. Thats right, ladies and gentlemen. I was allowed to make one of the biggest decisions of my life shortly after I learned to tie my shoes.

After gathering the courage to walk to the front of the auditorium while the older folks nodded with approval and pride, I sat and talked with a deacon who went through the whole baptismal mumbo jumbo. Ironically this was the same deacon, a man named Harry, who forcefully pinned my younger brother and me up against a brick wall some years later and wrongfully accused us of vandalizing the choir robes.

The baptismal ritual was as meaningless to me then as it is now and I can honestly say I only succumbed to the pressure of going through with it out of fear of going to hell. I certainly don't recall it making my soul feel cleaner or my heart feel fuller. It didn't result in the Almighty sending me a fancy car when I turned sixteen or helping me get better grades. On the contrary it may have scarred me for life. You see, as I was changing into the clothes I was to wear during the actual baptismal itself, I got my first glimpse of a grown man completely naked. It was horrendous. Pale, hairy, and out of shape, the image of this man dangling and flapping around the changing room is all I remember of the event.

As it turns out, dunking me under the surface of the water resulted in nothing more than a few bad dreams.

With age comes wisdom and the older I got the more I began to wonder about the whole concept of this thing called religion. What was the purpose of it? Why did some people go to one church to worship one god while others went to another? Even with all of this praying going on in the world I still saw poor people, heard about crime and violence, people still got sick and died, and the Cardinals didn't win the World Series every year. What was point?

The only impact religion had on me was that it made me fearful of things I now know to be harmless. For instance, I was so terrified God would punish me for masturbating that I didn't dare touch myself until I was fifteen years old. *Fifteen!* Can you believe that? My prepubescent years would have been so much easier if I hadn't had that guilt and shame hanging over my head and been worried about what Jesus thought of the tingling that was happening in my shorts. A boy has a right to feel comfortable enough with his own body to do what boys are supposed to do in the privacy of their bedrooms. We are born to make pages stick together and socks walk on their own. If we weren't meant to enjoy a little self gratification then why did our fathers save those old Playboy magazines in the basement? It's a right of passage and being a baptist robbed me of it.

When I finally lost my virginity to Kelly I honestly expected the world to explode on my way home. After all, we had enjoyed pleasures of the flesh out of wedlock and we all know what a crime against humanity that is. People have been stoned to death for such atrocities. Between my religious guilt and the fact that my mother had nearly walked in on us, I was a giant, sexually frustrated ball of emotional confusion.

My inquisitive nature reached a high point in my early twenties. I wanted answers. My search for the truth led me to read the Bible all the way through. Cover to cover. It meant so much to so many and I wanted to give it a fair shot. I felt there was no better way to fill in the philosophical blanks than to go right to the supposed source of creation.

If you have never read the Bible I highly suggest you do so. It is a remarkable work of fiction. A Google search will quickly identify the Bible as the bestselling book of all time, and with good reason. It has all a reader needs to stay compelled. The pages are filled with evil kings, magic, sorcery, sex, drama, intrigue, and intense male bonding. The male bonding refers to the twelve chaps that chose to give up their entire livelihoods, their jobs, their families, and their individuality in order to follow a man who appeared unto them claiming to be the son of God. Now, I work in Hollywood and I have come into contact with the smoothest talking devils who possess the slickest of tongues but I never, ever would've fallen prey to this kind of verbal splatter. The disciples, however, decided that earning a living and providing for their families could wait while they followed Jesus from village to village preaching eternal bliss. I'm not naming any names, or drawing any direct comparisons, but does this not remind you of acts other leaders in our history books have performed and been labeled as "tyrants" for?

As you become more and more enthralled with the tales the Good Book has to offer, you will be introduced to people who lived to be in their hundreds, a man who lived in the belly of a whale, an old fellow who, because of a voice from above, constructed a giant boat and filled it with two of every animal, and my personal favorite, a woman who had a baby without ever having sexual intercourse. The best part is... we are told that it is all *true!*

Today, thanks to a more educated and skeptical way of thinking, we are able to actually research things that raise questions in our minds. I have taken it upon myself to do just that.

Let us begin with Jonah. This poor guy. In the book of Jonah we learn that he was sent by God to a town called Ninevah. Apparently the Big Guy didn't like what the locals were up to there and summoned Jonah to head over and preach the good word in hopes of straightening them out. Jonah, being stubborn and fearful of the Ninevites, decided he'd pass on this assignment and instead hopped a boat to Tarshish-a town in the opposite direction. Well, as you can imagine, this really ruffled God's feathers. So much so that he caused a great and powerful storm that rocked the sea, causing the boat Jonah was on to be tossed among the mighty waves.

Allow me to pause here for a moment. Why would such a loving god put so many lives in danger if he was angry at only one man? And where is the forgiveness we're always hearing about? Couldn't he find another "fixer" to send to Ninevah?

Anyway, it turns out that Jonah showed compassion for the other people on the boat (even if God wouldn't) and confessed what he had done to cause the violent storm. He said the only way they could save themselves was by throwing him overboard in sacrifice. So, over he goes. Splash! His drowning is eminent...until! He is swallowed by a whale (or a big fish) that was sent by God. According to Jonah 2:9, Jonah lived inside of that whale for three days and three nights until he came to his senses and prayed for forgiveness.

FIrst of all, logic tells us that there's a very good chance Jonah would have been chewed up to some degree in order to fit down the whale's throat, right? A whale's digestive system starts with the tongue, then the esophagus, and continues down to the stomach which, like cows, consists of four chambers. Which chamber did Jonah camp out in? What did he do for nourishment? My best guess would be that he fed on partially digested fish. I cannot for the life of me, however, come up with a theory on how he found enough oxygen (under water) to stay alive for the thirty six hours it took for God to forgive him.

For Jonah not to have been absorbed and excreted must mean that the whale's digestive system stopped completely. Otherwise our hero would have, no doubt, become exactly what this whole fable is...a big pile of pure mammal dung.

I'd also like to touch on Abraham. By all standards, he was nothing more than a crazy old man who, at the age of 75, claimed to have had a vision from God that told him to lead his people to a better land. A noble undertaking, I'll admit. They agreed to follow him in mass numbers.

Abe had a rough go of it. Famine, intense weather conditions, run in's with some tough customers, and thousands of people constantly asking "Are we there yet?"

What really sends my skeptic meter off the charts on this one is the fact that Abe's wife, Sarah, passed away at the age of 127. What does Abraham do? Instead of enjoying bachelorhood for a while, he soon remarries and has six more sons. Let me get this straight. A man well into his hundreds is able to attract a new, young wife and have the desire, after this long life of doing God's work, to sire *six* more children without the help of those little blue pills we see the ads for on TV? Nope. Not buying it. From a scientific standpoint it just isn't conceivable. Even if he did reach that age (we are told he lived to be 175) there is not a man alive that would want a woman to touch him. He'd want nothing more than to be left alone in his Laz-Y-Boy while he waited for his next vision...or nap, whichever came first.

If you're not already nodding your head side to side in disbelief and wonder, this final example should seal the deal. It is the story of the virgin birth. Acknowledging that her husband, Joseph, must've been the ultimate king of denial, I offer this modern day scenario: A woman at your office, lets call her Mary, shows up one day and tells your boss that she is pregnant and will be needing maternity leave in the near future. No one knows Mary all that well but you do know that she is not married. She's never brought a boyfriend to any of the company events but she doesn't really seem like the slutty type, either. Yet here she is...in a family way.

As time goes on she begins to show and looks adorable. Everyone in the office caters to her every need as is usually the case until, one day, that nosey woman from HR finally asks the question that has been on all of your minds. Who is the father? With a coy grin, Mary explains that, although they were never intimate per say, God is the 'baby daddy.' You're stunned...waiting for her to say she is kidding. She's doesn't. She's serious. In an instant Mary goes from the sweet girl who is pregnant with her first child to that crazy chick who belongs on The Maury Povich Show.

I know many will read this and call me shallow for only focusing on the sexual inconsistencies of this beautiful tale, but if you want the juicy scientific stuff I suggest you read Richard Dawkins or Christopher Hitchens. Actually, I encourage you read them both because they are geniuses and science must, at the very least, be considered when deciding on the role religion will play in society.

And what about those previously mentioned disciples? Are we to believe they went on the Jesus Tour and never shared company with with the countless groupies that must have been throwing themselves at their washed feet? I'm not buying it. They had All Access passes to the man that could heal the sick so I am sure there were women willing to do anything to get close to him. *Anything.* I've seen women get creative just to get backstage at my shows and I'm only a game show host. I can't even imagine what it must be like for a guy who can turn water into wine.

The question must be asked, why would a god one who loves us so very much make the act of procreation so amazingly wonderful on so many levels and then also make it terrifying? I will never understand that.

I've never been a sleep around kind of guy. I enjoy being with one woman at a time and developing relationships that consist of more than just sweating and groaning. Women are beautiful specimens-all in your own way. I'm the father of a wonderful little girl that I absolutely cherish so I have respect for every woman. Alone time with a lady is one of the greatest things in the world and should not be scorned upon.

Most people I know enjoy sex. Come to think of it, most people I *don't* know enjoy sex. Very much, in fact. Why, then, does religion make it off limits unless you have taken the vow of marriage? Why is it considered a sin? Why not teach responsibility rather than abstinence? We are not the ones who made it so pleasurable, though some of us do put more effort into it than others. If it is meant solely as a mechanical process for reproduction then it shouldn't be so deeeeee-lightful. Thank you, your honor.

I declared myself an atheist shortly before Mason was born in 2001. My ex-wife, Silver, was always agnostic and I respected her opinions though never actually took them on as my own. I actually never really thought about it much until the question came up of how we were going to raise Mason when it came to religion. I knew, even before he was born, that I would never lie to him. That I would always be there for him when he needed guidance or had questions about anything. With the newfound focus that parenthood brings to one's life, I knew that I could never expect him to believe what the Bible tells us just *because*. What would I say when he asked questions? For some reason, telling him that he just had to have faith wasn't enough.

This caused me to look at my own beliefs. When I did that, when I really took the time to honestly ask myself what I believed to be true, the answer was very clear. I did not, and had not for a very long time, believe anything that religion or church had taught me. The stories I'd been spoon fed for so many years are not unlike the stories I would eventually read to my children. They all have colorful characters, a conflict, and seemed to end with a good, moral lesson that, if followed, will lead to a happy existence.

What's interesting about atheism is that when you begin to share your beliefs, or lack thereof, you quickly find others that are in the same boat and have been reluctant to say so. It's a shame that the believers are welcome, even encouraged, to be so vocal about their faith yet atheists are somehow looked at as Satan's children. I don't believe in a devil anymore than I believe in a god. I don't believe in any higher power at all. Sure, I fully acknowledge that I could be wrong, but what I believe is that we are born by natural, scientifically proven methods, we live for as long as we can, and then we die. When we do pass away there is no heaven or hell. We simply cease to exist. Hopefully our spirits live on in the form of memories that those who are near and dear to us carry with them and pass on to future generations. My goal is to treat people (and the planet) with respect and to love my family until my last breath. When that day comes, so be it. No one lives forever. Come to think of it, no one even lives to 175!

That leads me to the next point regarding death, dying, living, and surviving. It is our right and our responsibility to live the fullest life possible. Work hard to make your dreams come true. Love with all your heart. Laugh until your stomach hurts. But know that when it is over its *really* over. There isn't anything waiting for you "on the other side." There has never, ever been one solid ounce of proof that an afterlife exists. There are no brochures featuring mansions on streets of gold. The puppy you received for your fifth birthday is not waiting for you at the pearly gates. When your ticker stops ticking *that is it*!

This means that I absolutely, positively, without the slightest bit of hesitation or shadow of doubt do not believe in psychics, mediums, faith healers, fortune tellers, or anyone else toting a pair of crystal balls. These scam artists are nothing more than performers and predators skilled in tapping into the gullibility and weaknesses of others. They take advantage of those who have lost loved ones and need something to hold onto.

Successful mediums such as Sylvia Browne, James Van Pragh, the Long Island Medium, and John Edwards make a handsome living and have become celebrities by contriving a make believe link between those of us here on earth and those on "the other side." The problem is that there is no other side. I hate mentioning John by name because he and I worked together at HSN a few years ago and he seems like a very nice guy. He's even a big *Whammy!* fan. But I just cannot look past the fact that he takes money from people who quite often cannot afford it while providing nothing of real value in return.

I humbly admit that two arguments can be made for what I have just written and I shall address each of them. The first argument is how can I be so sure these individuals do not possess the supernatural, paranormal, hocus pocus powers they claim to? The answer to that is simple. If dead people were indeed able to communicate with the living we all have at least one person who would have contacted us. For me it would have been Nana.

Nana loved me more than anything in the world. She told me and she showed me. My mom loves Mason and Kiki that way. Your grandma probably loves you that way. If there was even the slightest possibility that she could communicate with me after her passing she would have done it by now. Nothing would have stopped her. And her communication would not have been in the form of a book falling off of a shelf or a medium asking me what the letter R represents. It would be a full on conversation that did not require me to piece anything together and left no doubt in my mind that I had just spoken to Nana. It would happen frequently and she surely would not make me pay for it.

Why, when I watch these mediums and psychics in action, is it always such a struggle to interpret the message? Why is it such a mystery? Webster's dictionary defines communication as *"a verbal or written message"* or *"a process by which information is exchanged between individuals..."* When your husband asks you where his car keys are you don't respond with an unsolvable riddle or a line from a movie. It's complete nonsense yet so many people so desperately want it to be true that they don't allow for any other possibilities.

I was recently in Ft. Lauderdale, FL, and had the great pleasure of spending time with James "The Amazing" Randi. Randi, to me, is an icon and a legend in the world of skeptical thinking and calling humbug (a more respectful way of saying *bullshit*) on those who need it called upon them the most.

Randi began his career as a magician and an escape artist and went on to achieve great popularity through appearances on *The Tonight Show with Johnny Carson* and countless other programs. But Randi became a household name when he stepped up and publicly challenged Uri Geller.

In the 1970's, Geller brought his act to America and claimed to have powers that allowed him to, among other things, bend spoons. Obviously there is nothing wrong with a magician or an illusionist performing their act for entertainment purposes, but Randi took offense to the fact that Uri claimed his powers were real and set out to prove to the masses that Geller was indeed a fake.

Randi organized demonstrations, both public and private, that did not allow for Geller or his entourage to prepare in advance. As a result, Geller suffered one failed experiment after another. The most devastating of which occurred on *The Tonight Show with Johnny Carson.* As a result of Randi's efforts, many now recognized Uri Geller for the fraud that he was.

Randi went on to tackle other shysters. Faith healers became a target for the Amazing one and he went on to expose many of their deceptive practices.

It was James Randi who exposed televangelist Peter Popoff's use of an earpiece to receive information about the members of his congregation. This was information that he claimed was provided by the Holy Spirit when, in fact, it was provided by Popoff's wife who was stationed in a secluded part of the tent with cameras, monitors, and a microphone.

Randi's books *The Truth About Uri Geller, Flim Flam, Faith Healers,* and others should be required reading for anyone who considers themselves to be a critical thinker.

Randi and I discussed many things, among them hypnotism and the importance of being a skeptic rather than a cynic. We shared a cup of coffee and wonderful conversation in his library. I cannot think of a more enlightening talk. The man is fascinating and I, like millions of others, am grateful for the work he and his organization, James Randi Educational Foundation (www.randi.org) continue to do to promote scientific inquiries into bogus claims.

With James "The Amazing" Randi at his home in Florida.

I bring Randi up for two reasons. One, to introduce you to him if you've never been made aware of the great work he does. And two, to tell you of his 1 Million Dollar Challenge. Randi's foundation, James Randi Educational Foundation, has a standing challenge to anyone who claims to possess paranormal or otherwise supernatural powers. If these powers can be proven by reasonable and scientific standards, that individual will receive one million dollars. Simple as that. This challenge has been made publicly to the likes of Sylvia Brown, who appears regularly on Montel Williams' show and in theaters around the world, yet the money still sits in the bank.

On the very same day of meeting Randi, a woman approached me at a restaurant while I was having dinner with a friend. She had attended a recent performance of mine in a local casino. She was very nice, probably mid forties, but very boisterous. It turns out she had lost her son to leukemia a few years before and I suspected she put on this loud exterior to mask the unimaginable pain she must still be feeling inside.

Like many people I meet after an event, she just needed to unload. I'm fine with that. I'm an unloader myself. And, although I'm not a therapist and I don't feel its my place to offer advice, I do believe that sometimes it just helps to let it out. As a parent myself, I don't even want to think about what she must have gone through during the long months of her son's sickness. I can't think of anything more devastating than watching your child suffer. I don't think there is a single one of us who wouldn't trade places with our kids if they were hurting. Sadly, life doesn't give us that option.

She went on and on until finally she said something to which I could no longer just stand by and nod sympathetically. She told me she went to a medium twice a month just so she could speak to her son.

Hearing her say that nearly made me spit up my chilean sea bass. There is a medium out there who knows this woman's pain, probably better than anyone, has watched her shed tears of the deepest sorrow, yet continues to charge her money for leading her to believe the six year old boy wants to communicate. Unbelievable, isn't it?

Does this medium smirk and chuckle every time the woman leaves her store? Does she feel so confident that this woman will be back time after time that she factors that money into her monthly budget? Does she say "Boy, I've got a live one on the hook," to other mediums?

I put my hand up to pause her train of thought. She looked at me with complete disbelief as I told her I do not believe in the afterlife and, if an afterlife did exist, I do not believe our deceased loved ones would chit chat with us in this way. They live on in the smiles that come to our faces when we think of them.

I knew this caused a little sting with her but I could not help myself. She was being stripped of her money and made to look like a fool. She even went as far as to tell me that her son wanted her to know that she had had over six hundred lives and will have six hundred more and they would eventually reunite in one of them.

She said she wanted me to meet her medium and I told her my email address is posted all over the internet. Have her get in touch. I also suggested she send her medium to Randi and take a shot at the million bucks. I've yet to receive an email and I bet Randi's cash has never been safer.

The second argument that can be made regarding my distaste, distrust, and dislike of supernatural superstars is the question of whether or not the psychics are providing a sense of satisfaction to those who are paying them. I believe they are. But that is not a moral or ethical argument.

Even though I think marijuana should be legalized, regulated, and taxed, isn't a drug dealer simply providing a service when he sells crack to a teenager who overdoses as a result? Even though I believe prostitution should be legalized, regulated, and taxed, isn't a hooker simply providing a service to man who neglects his wife and children to be with her? Technically speaking, all of these individuals are providing some sort of service. Utilizing those services, however, come with consequences.

If you've ever been to a psychic I can guarantee that, along with being in a shady part of town, you did not see a sign in the front room that read *"All Readings Are For Entertainment Purposes Only."* These people are very, very good and very, very intuitive. They ask the right questions and narrow your reading down to specifics based on your reactions-both verbal and non verbal. As James Randi said during our conversation, people want this information to be true so badly that they begin to *need* it to be true. Therefore they make it true in their own minds regardless of how many "misses" the psychic may have actually had before hitting on something. The same can be said for evangelists who take money from senior citizens on fixed incomes in return for prayer requests.

I can recall watching my grandmother write checks to Billy Graham as he shed tears of love and devotion on the television screen. Oral Roberts, Jimmy Swaggart, Pat Robertson, Jim Bakker, Joel Osteen, all the way back to Percy Crawford, they are all multi-millionaires who are cut from the same unholy cloth. They use the broadcast airwaves that I love so dearly as a tool to pull at your heart strings and grab at your wallet.

Sadly, the same can be said for many of my life coaching peers. People with failed marriages (guilty!), unsuccessful careers, less than ideal values, and poor health who sit at home and "coach" others while collecting anywhere from $200-$1,000/month. You want to see more money in your bank account? Here's a free coaching tip...don't waste your money on a bogus life coach and don't send it to a preacher.

I proved my point in 2002.

My ex-mother-in-law is a fascinating woman. Incredibly beautiful, lively, and artistically gifted, but also a believer in astrologers, fortune tellers, and the like. I decided to take it upon myself to debunk the theories she held true and it only cost me $65 and a few hours to do it.

She'd recently had her palm read and was fascinated by the accuracy of the results. After a short conversation in which I was unsuccessful in my attempt to show her the light, I went out to the local bookstore and purchased a small "How To" book on palm reading, or Palmistry, as it is known. It is far from a science. Essentially it consists of little more than interpreting what the lines in your hand have to say about your personality, love life, financial well being, health, etc.

Assuming that the lines on the bottom of our feet are as unique to us as the lines on our hands, I set out to sell the world on what I termed "Pedalogy."

Notice the spelling. A foot specialist is known as a podiatrist but I intentionally spelled the word so that it would more resemble the pedals on a bicycle. I did this wondering if those who truly wanted to believe would catch the ridiculousness of it. No one ever brought it up.

I ordered a box of custom pens that read *"Pedalogy...what do your feet say about you?"* and sent them, along with a letter of introduction, to a few radio personalities that I knew personally. These people had no idea the package was coming from me as the packages were sent using a different name. In the letter, I briefly described the new "science" using language from the palm reading book and offered to do free "readings" for the hosts and their listeners.

Within a couple of weeks, I had letters from radio stations across the country wanting to book me for interviews. In response, I requested clear photocopies of the bottom of one foot, whichever foot the individual favored, and vowed to reveal the results of my readings live on the air.

Soon my post office box was filled with requests from professional broadcasters who had found the time in their busy day to remove one shoe and balance themselves while propping one foot on the Xerox machine.

Disguising my voice with the poorest of English accents, I did radio interview after radio interview and astonished listeners with my "accuracy." During one particular call to a former competitor of mine in St. Louis, I asked my then mother-in-law to listen in on a three way line. I could hear her snickering as callers thanked me and repeatedly told me how "dead on" I was with my reading. I never so much as glanced at a single photo.

These listeners needed the lines on their feet to give them guidance and, by golly, toe jam covered guidance is what they got. My point was made, and "Pedalogy" faded off into the sunset.

Another brush with paranormal fluffery fell into my lap in early April of 2012.

I had just stepped off an overnight flight home from an event in Lake Charles, LA, when a text message came through from a fellow skeptic and writing partner of mine. In the message was a link to an article that instantly made my blood begin to boil. A twenty four year old "psychic" named Tiffany Smith (a.k.a. Sophie) had been arrested the day before in my hometown on charges of larceny and conspiracy. Her hearing was set for that very morning.

I read the entire article as I waited for my luggage to arrive on the carousel. According to the police report, Tiffany had been seeing a sixty nine year old client on a regular basis over the course of several months. The client, or more accurately, the victim, had recently become a widow and was seeing Tiffany in search of some form of comfort.

After accumulating enough information about the victim during previous visits, Tiffany went in for the kill. She told the woman that she was under "a black cloud...a curse" and only Tiffany could remove it. What is the going rate for having a curse lifted off of you, you ask? $16,000! What you're feeling as you read this is what I felt. Disgust, anger, and disbelief. But wait, there's more. Tiffany went on to tell the victim that if she chose not to have the curse lifted, the woman's daughter would eventually commit suicide. To emphasize the point, she threw a red liquid onto the ground to symbolize the blood of her daughter.

The woman, now terrified beyond belief, returned a few days later with a check for $7,000 (which was immediately cashed) and an antique ring worth $500. Tiffany pushed the woman to sell items and do all she could possibly do to raise the remaining $9,000. All the while reminding her of the doom awaiting the innocent and unsuspecting daughter. Luckily, the woman's son-in-law found out what had been happening and called the police. The police picked Tiffany up at her home, which was also her place of business (go figure).

Coincidentally, I'd been working on an idea for a new show called *Scam Slammers* for several months and was just waiting for the perfect case to come along to use in my pitch. Bingo! I'd found it. I grabbed my camera and raced to the courthouse to see if I could get an interview with "Sophie the Psychic" herself.

I had no sooner gathered my belongings from the x ray conveyer belt and passed through security when I spotted her in the lobby. A short, pudgy girl with the worst hair dye job you can imagine. Think Sylvia Browne only younger. She was talking to two other women. One I took to be her mother and the other appeared to be the public defender that had been assigned to the case. I got as close as I could but it was difficult to hear what they were saying over the clanging of the gaudy gold hoops dangling from her ears.

A local reporter sat next to me and asked who I was covering the story for. I think she thought E! had taken an interest in psychics. I explained what I was up to and she loved it. We spoke for a bit longer before noticing Tiffany's mother heading for the front door. If I couldn't interview Tiffany I would go for the next best thing-the beast that bore her.

The reporter signaled her cameraman to follow us outside. I politely asked her to let me ask the questions as I could afford to be a little more forward and gruff than she could. If her cameras were rolling, she'd still get all the soundbites. She agreed and stayed right on my heels as I followed the mother out to the parking lot.

I caught up to her just as she reached her car. She turned at the sound of my voice and immediately noticed the cameras. The shocked expression on her face was priceless and I immediately began firing the questions at her.

"Are Tiffany's psychic powers real?"

"Are you proud of your daughter for scamming an old lady out of her life savings?

"If a curse costs $16,000 to be lifted, how much to find out who will win the World Series?"

She had nowhere to go and threw her hands up to hide her face. The dream shot! She denied that her daughter was a psychic, or even a reader, and insisted the victim was making the whole thing up. I could not have written a better line for her to say because later that afternoon I went by Tiffany's home and shot video footage of a giant sign in her front yard that said **PSYCHIC**, as well as signs in the windows that read **SPIRITUAL READINGS**.

After getting what we needed in the parking lot, the reporter and I went back inside. I watched the frazzled mother return and relay what had just happened outside to Tiffany. I held her stare as she looked over at me. She blinked first. I won the showdown.

Moments later her case was called. I was two steps behind Tiffany as she entered the courtroom. Unfortunately, no cameras were allowed inside. I took a seat less than three feet from where she stood while the prosecuting attorney read the charges against her and went through the testimony of the victim's family. Though she didn't look over at me once, my eyes never left her and I could tell she felt my glare. When the judge announced her bail at $1,500 her head dropped. I whispered, "Gotcha."

As of this writing, Tiffany is awaiting trial. Regardless of the final verdict and what punishment she may face, another psychic is off the streets. There are many more, but one step at a time. The good guys won in Massachusetts that day.

Look, I would love for there to be a giant Happily Ever After for all of us. I think, as a whole, we deserve to have a big pot of gold at the end of this rainbow we call life. For those who really need it, I would also like for there to be a proven method of predicting what is waiting around the corner. I personally have no wish to know what my future holds. I love the spontaneity of life, but I respect that peeking into the unknown would lift the burdens of fear and worry for many. But it just doesn't work that way, and no amount of wanting it to work that way is going to make it so.

On the contrary, unfounded faith might actually hurt. You don't have to be a historian to know of the ill side effects of religion or the awful lengths the devoted have gone to in the name of their gods. All you really have to do is visit the World Trade Center memorial site or read about the Holocaust. I'm not stating that religious people are bad, I'm saying the basis on which organized religion was founded is outdated, unhealthy, and counterproductive to modern society.

We are no longer an uneducated and illiterate group of lemmings that needs fear and guilt to corral us into proper order. We are well informed and generally compassionate human beings who, at the core, all want the same thing...peace and happiness for all mankind. So, as I gently hum the melody of "Jesus Loves Me" to myself, I offer this. Maybe, just maybe, the world is due for a biblical rewrite. Oh, wait... the Mormons already tried that.

CHAPTER 8
AMERICA'S LIFE COACH

A coach is someone who tells you what you don't want to hear, who has you see what you don't want to see, so you can be who you have always known you can be.
-Tom Landry, legendary coach of the Dallas Cowboys

ANYONE WHO IS *NOT* constantly looking for the BBD (Bigger Better Deal) is operating at a level a little south of sanity. You may have a college degree (or two) or an IQ that is off the charts, but if you aren't constantly scanning the horizon looking for a way to take that next leap you're shortchanging yourself and your family.

There is no excuse for moving horizontally and it should be feared just as much as moving backwards. Our minds are programmed to move forward so you must decide if you're hopping aboard the train or staying behind and cleaning toilets at the station. You're either the hammer or the nail...its up to you when the pounding starts.

People of our generation will never know what it is like to go home every night knowing that our jobs will more than likely be there for us for as long as we want them. Not only is that a prehistoric way of thinking, but it falls under the category of Fantasy. Forget job security. In this day and age you need to rely on yourself and no one else. That is not to say we are alone in this world. Far from it. But no one is as passionate about your dreams as you are.

In 2008, the Bureau of Labor Statistics stated that the average American worker stays with an employer for 4.1 years. What happens then? Do they get fired? Quit? Start their own business? The definition of a career change is fuzzy, but what is more than clear is that we all shed our skin and take on new shapes. Personally, I've been a pizza delivery boy, radio DJ, TV host, life coach, speaker, a hypnotist, and I'm just getting started! Rare is he who finds employment so perfectly suited to his talents and goals that it spans an entire career. I know of only one example. My high school friend, Tony.

In school Tony was a good looking cat. He did much better with the girls than I did, which really isn't saying much. He played football, had a great sense of humor, was a bit of a trouble maker, and was always part of the "in crowd." I liked him a lot.

When we were juniors at Oakville High, most of us went out and got jobs because being cool has never been free. Being a pizza delivery driver was considered a pretty sweet gig for a kid with a newly obtained driver's license so I did that for awhile before going in search of real cash and excitement. That job certainly had its perks. I got to work with my buddies, got all the pizza I could eat, and had the freedom to swing by my girlfriend's house when business was slow. Other than my car constantly smelling of sausage and onions it wasn't too bad.

Tony opted to work at a grocery store. It was a local chain where he started off the way everyone does, as a bagger. He worked his way up to stock boy and, over time, continued on up the ladder. I don't know a thing about how the grocery industry works so that's as far as I can take you. But I do know that Tony is now enjoying a nice management position in that same company. I'm sure he has a 401k, nice benefits for his family, and no problem affording the payments on the home he purchased just a few miles from where we grew up. Some would say he's living the dream and I am very happy for him.

But Tony's dream is my nightmare.

I've always loved what I've done for a living. Otherwise I wouldn't have done it in the first place. There have been some jobs that I've grown not to love, some that I have found disappointing to some degree, and others that I have simply outgrown. But, all in all, I have found something valuable from each and every endeavor. Many times this nugget has been that the position or project turned me on to a new passion or allowed me to uncover a new path in my career.

A perfect example of this is when I worked at Burger King. I was fifteen years old and and it took me all of three hours to nearly turn the place into a raging inferno because I didn't drain the grease out of the fryer properly. Fortunately, the manager was able to subdue the flames in time to serve a bus load of hungry senior citizens the crisp, golden fries they so craved.

I learned two things on that fiery night: First, my place in a fast food restaurant is in front of the counter, not behind it. And secondly, you never throw water on a grease fire. At least I now knew where I *didn't* belong. It was time to seek out a place where my true calling could come to life and my talents would be put to better use.

From this quest to find the BBD, America's Life Coach was born.

I'm often asked how I came to be known as America's Life Coach. To the disappointment of many, it's a simple story.

In December of 2009, I was delivering a keynote speech to a Fortune 500 company at the Marriott Hotel in downtown San Diego. At the conclusion of my presentation, I ran offstage after the presentation and, together with my assistant Carmendy, rushed to the airport to catch a plane to Las Vegas for another speech that was to begin in less than three hours.

Commenting more on the craziness of the day's schedule than the actual content of my presentation, my Carmendy said, "Two speeches in two different cities in less than five hours. Man, you're America's Life Coach!"

It definitely had a ring to it and was still stuck in my head as I went to my hotel room later that evening. I bought the domain, had my graphics designer create a logo, and the rest is impulsive, ego-driven history.

Now whenever I speak or do an interview promoting an appearance, I request to be introduced as America's Life Coach. It's not a title, it's actually nothing more than a nickname, but repetition builds reputation and, along with providing a powerful and valuable message through my speaking engagements, the name has stuck.

Delivering The Choice Is Yours in New York, NY. 2010.

There's nothing sexy about that story. There's also nothing exotic about the way I became so deeply involved in the field of personal development and human achievement.

My tale is not as dramatic as the stories other coaches and speakers would like you to believe their stories to be. Truth be told, there are quite a few snake oil salesmen (and women) out there who think that just because their friends in the cul de sac come to them for generic makeover tips or advice on how to spice up their loveless marriages they should become a "life coach."

Todd Newton

In this day and age just about anyone can design a website and market themselves as a "guru" or an "expert." Sadly, for those who spend their hard earned money on these people in hopes of a flash of enlightenment, these "coaches" are not equipped with the tools needed to produce real results. Why? Because coaching requires skill and training. It is a valid and respected profession. None of these fly-by-nighters would dare to step on a little league baseball field and give eleven year old Timmy pointers on how to hit a curveball. It's not what they do. Yet they feel qualified to assist someone who has a communication breakdown with a spouse that could result in the demise their relationship.

The personal development industry has become increasingly popular in the last decade. Movie stars, CEO's. athletes, and artists love to talk publicly about the breakthroughs they've had with their coaches, the latest book they've read, or the seminar that changed their life.

In this time of economic uncertainty, increased divorce, unemployment, technological advancement, and overwhelming opportunity, confusion seems to be running rampant. People want to change careers but don't know how. Parents want to bond with their children but don't know how. Baby boomers want to stay in the workforce but don't know how. It can be frightening but fear only comes from not knowing. You're only afraid to walk into a dark room because you can't see what is inside. Once you turn the light on all panic disappears. The same can be said about your life's journey. Once a qualified coach joins you and assists you in "turning on the light," your fear shifts to optimism. Optimism creates excitement. Excitement creates momentum. Momentum creates action. And action creates results! My desire to coach, and coach effectively, led me to write the following article that appeared in my blog in January of 2012.

Everyone Is A Life Coach...NOT!

Yes, I know. To end a sentence with a giant, capitalized NOT is very 1992 and reminds us all of a time when Pearl Jam was selling out arenas and Lethal Weapon movies were on the marquee of the local theater. But let's face it, we all know what it means and, just like No Whammies Big Bucks (sorry, shameless plug), it may be a bit out of date but it will never lose its meaning.

I was inspired to write this article after a recent discussion with two of my colleagues in the personal development/health & wellness field. Both of these women possess a drive and an inner light that have *quickly drawn me to them and I jumped at the opportunity to join them for a late dinner on a recent chilly night in New England.*

As we sat around the candlelit table enjoying a bottle of red wine, the conversation naturally turned toward what led us all into doing what we did for a living. One of the women, lets call her Anne, had studied science and metaphysics and developed a fascination with the way the universe and, everything and everyone in it, are connected. She pursued this interest by studying everything from yoga to meditation to massage. As I sat and listened to her plans to travel to Thailand to study further and eventually create an all natural resort that will benefit the locals as well as tourists, I fell in love with her passion and immediately became grateful for this newfound connection.

The other woman, we shall call her Elizabeth, is a massage. She is the mother of three and has one of the most radiant and permanent smiles I believe I have ever seen. And that means a lot coming from a game show host! I label her smile as beautiful not only because she has perfect teeth but because it is genuine. During her bodywork sessions she pays close attention to all aspects of the clients energy. Her mission during each therapeutic hour is not only to work out the kinks in your neck but to relax and rejuvenate your mind, body, and spirit.

I loved hearing about the paths that brought them to where we all now sat. They shared a long friendship and it was a joy to watch them work off of each other in practice and in conversation. When it came to be my turn to talk about Todd Newton Life Strategies and how I got into personal development, I told the story that I have told many times in interviews, to clients and to colleagues. Its really nothing special. I never hit rock bottom. I never lost it all only to regain it. I've never been so moved by a guru that I felt the need to give back to my fellow man. I've simply always found great strength through speakers, authors, and mentors and felt I had the beginnings of becoming one myself. I love all aspects of my life and believe in the philosophies that have gotten me to where I am. Focus, family, hard work, integrity, compassion, self-reliance, continuous effort, and instincts are what I practice as well as what I preach. After reaching a point where I had concrete evidence of these beliefs providing positive outcomes in my own life, I felt compelled to offer them to others who might also find them to be of use.

Being a TV personality has given me a bit of a jump start over others in that I had a built in platform. You see, when I decided I wanted to do this I knew I wanted to be the best. Most of us consider the same names to be the top of the heap with it comes to motivation and inspiration. Names like Tony Robbins, Jim Rohn, Wayne Dyer , Steven

Covey, and countless others are the MVPs of this game. I've always been most moved by Tony. I first listened to his tapes and CDs in my early 20's. I connected with him because we both spent a large portion of our bachelorhoods in Venice Beach, CA. I have great admiration for how he has turned motivation into an empire. He takes some heat for being "too commercial" but I think its that very packaging that has exposed millions of people to his work that otherwise may never have stumbled upon it. When I attended my first Tony Robbins seminar in Las Vegas, NV, I knew instantly that I was going to one day electrify stages in the same fashion. Now I do. Being on television certainly doesn't hurt when it comes to booking speaking engagements and gathering Google hits.

Whatever Tony did I was going to do. I'm not copying him or imitating him...I'm modeling his process. When someone is doing something you want to do and doing it well it makes perfect sense to follow their patterns. Tony preaches this very tactic. Tony studied the framework and techniques of effective coaching. I became a certified coach and acquired those same skills. Tony is a Master NLP practitioner and utilizes its many aspects in his seminars. I am a Master NLP practitioner and have seen the benefits of anchoring and changing emotional states in more clients than I can count. Tony mixes in a little conversational hypnosis when on stage in front of a sold out arena crowd. I'm an advanced clinical hypnotherapist who is still waiting to get booked at Madison Square Garden-but I am working on it. Tony is a marketing genius who has positioned himself as the "The Man" in personal development. Most importantly, Tony cares and wants everyone to be a happy and productive human being. I think we all can come together on that one.

And that brings me to the point of this article. If you're reading this then perhaps you are a coach yourself. I'm sure you are passionate and more than qualified to assist your treasured clients on their journeys to greatness. I'm certain that you are continuously reading about new coaching techniques, attending seminars, building your brand, networking with other coaches and furthering our multi-million dollar industry in the most respectful and professional of ways. If this is you, then you are who I am writing TO. On the flip side, if you are someone who got a wild hair one day and decided that Tweeting quotes by Thoreau and Mother Theresa qualifies you to charge people hundreds of dollars a month just to chat with you on the phone then you are who I am writing ABOUT.

Don't get me wrong. I love living in a country where we all have the liberty and luxury to pursue any career we choose. Becoming a life coach is a noble calling and one that should be taken on with great respect and responsibility. A respect not only for the craft of coaching but also for those who will one day become clients that depend on us to know what we are doing.

We all agree that we are not therapists, consultants, or counselors. What many who enter our field seem to be confused by is that we are also not meant to be advice givers. I once met a woman who decided she was going to add "life coach" to a resume that included image expert, entrepreneur and author. After getting to know her a little better, I came to realize that although she had started a couple of businesses she had lost them both due to poor management and a lack of entrepreneurial vision. Her experience as an image expert included little more than talking with her girlfriends about what she thought looked good in the latest issue of Vogue Magazine. And, as an author, she has yet to publish a single piece of work. Now, with time on her hands and a need for additional income, she had decided to...drumroll please... become a life coach!

There are countless outlets where one can receive coach training and certifications. They come in different ranges of tuition and offer different schedules to fit any lifestyle. Whether one is better than the other is a matter of opinion, but I thoroughly enjoyed my training and pointed her in the same direction I had gone. I also passed on a book title or two that I had found beneficial in building my practice. After several weeks I asked what type of training she planned on pursuing and was taken aback by her response.

"I'm not going to pay for training. It's pretty expensive. Besides, there's no right or wrong way to coach," she said.

That was it. Her mind was made up. She didn't need any instruction. She had no desire to work with established coaches. She updated her website, started Tweeting the typical rah-rah quotes, and fluffed her bio on the free listing sites with made up testimonials. Thus, a new life coach was born.

I don't fault this woman for taking such a laissez-faire approach to life coaching. Again, last time I checked it was still a free country. As a matter of fact, a job that you can do over the phone from your back porch or while you're strolling through the aisles at the grocery store probably sounds pretty darn good to just about anyone. But what about her clients? What about the young man or woman on a tight budget who just graduated from college and hires a coach in search of direction? What about the employee who feels stuck? What about the manager who wants to improve his leadership skills? They deserve more than a coach who feels qualified to assist anyone who answers her ad because "she's always been the one her friends came to for advice."

In the wonderful book "Talent Is Overrated," author Geoff Colvin stresses that no one is born great at anything. While some may have obvious advantages over others, greatness is achieved through what he refers to as "deliberate practice." This is what made Tiger Woods a great golfer. It's what made Beethoven a great composer. And it is what makes Tony Robbins a personal development superstar. Deliberate practice is finding exactly what needs to be learned and also precisely how to work on it. It's not easy. It requires what every good coach speaks of and lives with...PASSION.

My goal with this article is to encourage all of my fellow coaches to revisit and reignite your passion for what we do NOW. Before your next coaching call, close your eyes and put yourself into that powerful state that you were in when you first said to yourself, "Yes. This is something I was meant to do. I'm going to make a difference in lives of people I've never even met. I'm going to do this the right way!" Remember the rush you experienced the first time you heard a great speaker or the first time you had an "a-ha" moment with your own coach? That is passion and we must never lose it or take it for granted. It is that passion that sets us apart and serves as the key ingredient in those of us who have dedicated a part of our lives to becoming Life Changers and Dream Makers.

I do not believe in the concept of perfection. I believe that there is always room for growth, improvement, and learning. There are areas in my own life that I work on improving constantly. Today, I invite you to join me in making a commitment to always be the best coaches we can be. We are fortunate to work in an area where competition should not be present among each other but only within ourselves. Competition to be even better and more effective than we were on the last call.

Yes, I am proud and protective of our industry. I have shared those golden moments with clients and heard the magic of a shift in their voices. I do not rely on coaching as my main source of financial income. Not many do. A recent study of 3,000 coaches revealed that 70% of them earned less than $10,000 per year. I do, however, believe in the value of our services and have come to rely upon it as a source of emotional income.

No. Everyone is not a life coach. Nor is everyone a doctor, a landscaper, or a shoeshiner. I mean to offend or insult no one with this article. Instead I mean to inspire those I am writing ABOUT to find the passion to become one that I am writing TO.

Until we meet again on the road to your greatness...

There are some who would say a life coach is an advisor. I strongly disagree. I am no more qualified to give advice to you as you are to give it to me. I in no way mean for that to sound disrespectful or as an insult to your intelligence. I'm sure you are a wonderful human being with much to offer, but I take advice from very few. Unless you have absolutely mastered something that I absolutely want to master myself then your words are going to be lost on me. Don't tell me how to discipline my kids when you don't have children of your own. I have enough faith in my own instincts that I would rather work my own way through it. For example, if I feel that I need to improve on connecting with contestants while hosting a game show, I will go to Bob Barker or Sande Stewart and seek their advice on how the best way to achieve this. I would not be interested in the advice of, let's say, a chef or an astronaut. It's just not what they are qualified to speak on.

Many life coaches are the same way. They give relationship advice yet have not had a meaningful relationship to speak of. They give entrepreneurial advice yet the one business they started crashed and burned within a year. They give financial advice yet are literally living paycheck to paycheck. Again, I'm sure they are beautiful souls but they should not be advising others on key matters. Instead, a coach should assist you in creating options.

To reiterate what I wrote in the blog, a life coach is also not a therapist. One of the first things I learned while training and becoming certified as a coach was *coaching is not therapy.* Human beings are a complex species and I would never lead a potential client to believe that I am qualified to guide them out of serious depression, an abusive relationship, or some sort of dependency. That is what shrinks are for and anyone with that type of issue should find a therapist that can best serve them.

I made the distinction between coaching and therapy very clear in the first consultation-or "sample session" as it is often called. This abbreviated version of a coaching call is just as much for the client as it is for me. It's purpose is to see if we are a good fit for one another and for me to determine if I can be of significant assistance. If I couldn't help you I would not take your money. It's not that I didn't want your cash in my pocket. Believe me, I did. But more than that, I wanted my clients to succeed and to achieve all that they wanted and deserved. Integrity has no price tag.

Coaching was always meant to serve as a preamble to my keynote speaking career. The certifications, the NLP, and the hypnotherapy all were pursued solely to enhance my presentations. Non-verbal communication accounts for 90% of my message so I wanted to make sure I could effectively communicate even when I wasn't actually speaking.

This area of my career comes from an entirely different place. When I was hosting on E! from 1995-2007, I had the good fortune to serve as the master of ceremonies or guest speaker at countless events for our affiliates and advertisers. I always enjoyed these events as they gave me an opportunity to travel around the country and meet the people who were out there promoting our network on a daily basis. It also gave me the chance to do what I love doing which is talking into a microphone in front of a large crowd and being the center of attention.

For many years I would use my time on stage to talk about my experiences on the red carpet. People always want to know who my favorite (and least favorite) interviews have been. The truth is there are no bad interviews. In a red carpet or movie junket situation these highly paid stars are there for one reason-to promote what it is they're there to promote. They are on their best behavior but you're not going to become coffee buddies with someone after only sharing five minutes surrounded by screaming fans, nosey publicists, and television cameras. You may, however, end up with the phone number of a B movie actress. It's been known to happen.

I realized after speaking at several of these functions that my stories were beginning to feel stale to me. They weren't fun to tell anymore and it became difficult to muster up any enthusiasm with which to tell them. Dare I say I even began to *not* look forward to getting on stage. I couldn't afford for this to happen. At the time, I was getting $5,000-$10,000 a speech and that's not the kind of money you just turn down. I needed to make a shift. I needed to find a topic that I was passionate about and something that I knew the audience would benefit from. Something other than how good Julia Roberts' hair smells...and it smells *amazing*!

It was my dear friend Ken Botelho who advised me on sharing my background in the entertainment industry and the philosophies had led me to where I was at that point. At first I though he was insane. In fact, I though what every motivational speaker thinks at the beginning of their speaking career, *"Why would anyone want to hear my story?"* The answer was simply because I was the one on stage and the audience had nowhere else to go.

I began to think about how it did actually all begin. At what point did this fascination with being in the public eye kick in for me? The answer, I discovered, was around the age of thirteen.

I grew up watching people like Johnny Carson and Dick Clark. Men who made a living on the radio and on television just being themselves. This is what I wanted for myself for as long as I can remember. As I mentioned in an earlier chapter, I struck a deal with my parents that allowed me to listen to the radio in my room while I did my homework as long as my grades didn't suffer. This never became an issue because the only time I ever paid attention to what was coming through the speakers was in between the songs when the DJ would speak. I've always hated Top 40 music-even when I played it on the radio myself-but I've always *loved* a smooth talkin' DJ. It seems that all of the great hosts began their careers on the radio and I knew that was what I wanted to do if and when I ever grew up.

As the story goes, I did indeed become a popular DJ, which led to television, then on to the speaking. But the road has been far from smooth. I've been passed on, looked over, and put down. Yes, I've taken my share of hits along the way but I never stopped working toward my goal. There are no shortcuts and you can bet your old Ford pickup there is no such thing as an overnight success. Anyone who has anything has busted tail for it. Period. Unless your daddy hands power and prestige to you on a silver platter (George W. Bush) you've got to sweat it out down here with the rest of us.

I watched my father go to work everyday. I watched him start new businesses for himself and explore new opportunities. I watched him do everything a man should do to provide for his family while my mother stayed home and took care of us. My grandparents were close by so we were always surrounded by love and support. They all taught me to save my money for a rainy day but also that it was also okay to splurge a little now and then. They never once told me or my brother that something we wanted to achieve was out of our reach. That is the greatest gift a parent can give a child...belief.

Dreams do come true and they come true every single day. Today, my son Mason wants to be a hockey player when he grows up. Just this morning he hit the ice at 6:50am and scored two goals for his team. He's ten years old and can't imagine a future that doesn't include skates and scars. I'm at every game I can attend yelling, clapping, and banging on the glass for him and his team. I know he may find it embarrassing, but I'm so proud of that kid and I am behind him all the way. That's what parents do.

Another value that my midwestern upbringing instilled within me and that I speak of on stage is good, old fashioned honesty. Now, I'd be lying if I said I didn't learn the hard way that the truth is the *only* way. I know that I'm preaching to the choir because each and every one of us has been caught in a lie at some point in our lives and it isn't fun. It's humiliating, demoralizing, and it causes you to waste a lot of time backtracking in order to rebuild the trust.

Speak the truth, no matter how difficult it may seem, and you'll have much less to remember. Most people can smell a lie from a mile away and will steer clear of it. Sugarcoating and being "economical" with your straightforwardness will create more problems than they avoid. Be that person that everyone can rely on and you will see opportunities begin to pile up. On top of all this, being a truthful and authentic person leaves your heart feeling light and gives you an inner warmth. That feeling of knowing that you are genuine, that you have integrity, allows you to walk just a little bit taller than the rest of the herd.

Honesty, hard work, the ability to say 'no', a strong support group, a devotion to family, and a clear sense of direction...doesn't sound much different from your own story, right? You may be missing one or two of those key ingredients but I'm sure you've had a taste of them at some point or another. And I'm sure you will, with a little bit of work, have them again. But these are the factors that have played a major role in getting me to where I am today and I knew I now had a platform to share them with others through my speaking opportunities.

Not only did I have a forum, but I also had developed a niche. I targeted not only those groups and individuals looking to take the world by storm, but also those who just wanted to contentment. Success, as we know, means different things to different people and I wanted my presentations to reach the largest amount of the population as possible.

I have made my share of money over the years but I am not Warren Buffet. Personal development experts who spend a lot of time telling you how much money came their way through the use of a particular product or principle are usually winding up for the big sales pitch or the "Call To Action," as it sometimes called.

What I can honestly tell you is that, with virtually no job stress, I have made a great living doing what I love to do. I provide quite well for my family, have a good credit rating, and all my bills are paid. I'll also tell you that I've been accused of living far below my means. This may be true, but it sure beats the headaches that comes from living beyond them.

Another popular area in the self help genre is romance. Bookstores are full of books that focus on finding that special someone. People line up to purchase tickets to seminars that will teach them how to locate their soulmate. One must proceed with caution where the heart is concerned. Especially when that heart belongs to someone else.

I've had my share of relationships, but I am no expert on love. As I openly admit in the pages of this book, I've been involved with some of, what I consider to be, the most spectacular women in the world. Beautiful, intelligent, funny, sexy, well-traveled, and fascinating women that I've been fortunate enough to spend a portion of my days with. Like most relationships, they all ended. But from each one I learned valuable lessons.

I joke onstage when I say, "Falling in the love is the most beautiful thing in the world. That's why I do it so often." But there is a bit of truth to it. I believe in completely devoting myself to a relationship and seeing it through to the end, in being monogamous and, this is important, being honest about what and *who* I am. I'm not interested in short flings or one night stands because they don't contribute to the direction I want my life to take. That said, as an international speaker I now have those experiences from all of my past relationships to share with others from stages all over the world. No one can tell you where the person you'll be spending the rest of your life is having lunch today, but a good speaker can offer you some tried and true philosophies on how to prepare and make yourself more receptive when your paths eventually cross.

Not everyone seeks money or love. We all have different goals and identifying exactly what it is we want, as opposed to what we *don't* want, can be an important step in attaining it. Some goals are bigger than others but, regardless of the size, accomplishing something you've set out to do or attaining something you've set out to get results in a tremendous feeling of pride and accomplishment. Whether it's a new car, a new home, a new boyfriend, or a promotion at work, finally wrapping your fingers around the prize is a thrill beyond words.

Have I attained every goal I have set for myself? Not even close. If that were the case, I'd be the host of *The Tonight Show* and be married to the girl I sat next to in 7th grade Biology class. No one knocks it out of the park every time. Some of us rarely even put bat to ball. But you don't have to achieve everything to be identified as an achiever.

I believe that success can stem from knowing what doesn't work as well as what does.

In *The Choice Is Yours*, I speak on the difference between a goal and a dream. I once had a client come to me and say she dreamed of retiring, buying a yacht, and sailing around the world. Sounds incredible, doesn't it? It also sounds overwhelming and that is what was holding her back. Rather than offering her advice, we worked together to increase the number of choices she had in ways to make this a reality for her and her husband.

I asked my client to substitute the word *dream* with the word *goal*. Although it felt odd for her initially, it gave the whole image a clearer direction. It made everything a little more black and white.

As a result of now being able to put it all in better perspective, she concluded that she would work for 12 more months in order to add to her savings fund. This additional income would allow her to retire comfortably without financial concerns. With peace of mind, she and her husband would charter a boat (rather than buy a yacht) and sail the Mediterranean (rather than the *world*). It was something they had always talked of doing and by creating a roadmap to the desired destination, it was now going to happen.

In the summer of 2010, she left her cell phone at home and hit the high seas. Judging by the photos they sent me, it was paradise.

A results oriented life coach needs to be relatable to the client. A worthy speaker should inspire and guide through the words of his or her message. Think Abraham Lincoln, Winston Churchill, and Martin Luther King, Jr. Through my personal experiences, as well as this book, I hope to assist you in transforming your life from where you are *right now.*

Unlike traditional forms of therapy, which I am all in favor of if needed, coaching focuses on the present and the future rather than the past. On strategies rather than feelings. It's more about listening and learning to hear what the client is *really* saying.

A trained coach will open up new ways of thinking that allow you to improve your life in a countless ways...building strong relationships, changing or building your career, time management, goal setting, developing an overall life balance. Watching audience members as they begin to live their lives to the fullest became something that really turned me on. After going through what I hope was the darkest period of my life and coming out shining on the other side, I wanted to share that feeling of newfound joy with others. Becoming a lifelong student of personal development and having access to a large audience seemed to be the ticket.

I started looking around at those who were dominating the speaking world. In addition to Tony Robbins, I'm sure you've heard the names T.

Harv Ecker, Jack Canfield, and John C. Maxwell. These are the big boys. The heavy hitters. These are the names that are attracting thousands of people to seminars and selling millions of books...and pocketing millions of dollars in the process. But, in my opinion, they are also the real deal. They wouldn't be so successful if what they were offering didn't work. They are masterful coaches, authors, and speakers and I was going to join their ranks come hell or high water.

We don't call it copying. That's a word reserved for when a school kid peaks at his classmate's paper and writes down the same answers. What I did is called *modeling*, which essentially means you reproduce the behavior or actions that have proven to be successful for others.

Tony Robbins is the man that I chose to emulate. As a matter of fact, the great organization Toastmasters International published an article in their monthly magazine that touched on the similarities between the two of us that I found incredibly flattering (*Don't Hesitate-Emulate. November, 2011*).

Tony usually wears black on stage-I *always* wear black on stage. Tony is a life coach. I became a certified life coach (*Coach Training Alliance*). Tony utilizes NLP "Neurolinguistic Programming) in his presentations. I became a Master NLP Practitioner and Trainer (*Life Potential Developments*). Tony utilizes conversational hypnosis. I studied and became an advanced clinical hypnotherapist (*New England Institute of Hypnotherapy*). If I ever find out what kind of toothpaste Tony uses, you can bet I'll rush out and buy the same brand.

I modeled Tony's behavior because he is a winner. What he does, and the way he does it, works. I began to blend my unique style with a message that would benefit many. I was building myself into a master presenter. An info-tainer. An orator with swagger.

Fortunately, during this period in 2008, I had the time to invest in my new passion. I had signed a contract with HSN (Home Shopping Network) that meant I would be commuting from Los Angeles to Tampa on a weekly basis. I don't know if that would be the right move for me today, but at the time it was exactly what I needed to do...professionally and personally.

Professionally, I had devoted most of my working days to hosting *The Price Is Right Live!* stage show in Las Vegas and various other cities around the country in hopes of positioning myself as the logical choice to replace the great Bob Barker when he retired. It was the right thing to do, and I love hosting that show to this day, but the traveling took me out of the running for a lot of auditions and television projects that were currently in production.

On the personal side of things, Silver and I had just split and I had taken an apartment a mile or so from her and the kids. We never had any disagreements about who should have primary custody of the children. If the mother is loving and respectable then the kids belong with her the majority of the time, but it would have been too difficult for me emotionally to know that my babies were just around the corner on the days we didn't spend together. Hopping on a cross country Delta flight to sell toaster ovens seemed like a good way to keep myself busy until I could see them again. Plus, it was *really* good money and I needed the paycheck.

After doing some research, I discovered that an organization out of Colorado called Coach Training Alliance offered solid training that I could complete online and through teleseminars. In addition to the key skills of coaching, CTA would teach me business skills, marketing tips, and provide me live one on one training and exercises with mentors and fellow students. Perfect...sign me up!

I ate this learning up like a $5 buffet. That is to say I couldn't get enough. The more I learned about the process of coaching, and the many different techniques that have been designed to help others, the more I knew these skills would lead to powerful speeches.

I would get off the air at HSN, grab a quick bite to eat, and hit the books. I began coaching everyone I came into contact with. Some people loved it while others thought it was voodoo nonsense. I started marketing my coaching on the social media sites (which I believe, for the most part, are completely worthless) as well as through word of mouth with my Hollywood friends and had a client list established before I had even completed the course.

No two of my coaching clients were the same and not everyone who contacted me for coaching was the right fit, but through my training I had developed a network of other coaches that I felt comfortable referring people to. As my client roster grew so did my fascination.

Speaking at an event in Miami, FL. 2012.

Coaching kept me pretty busy throughout 2008 and 2009, but I felt as if I was hitting just shy of the goal. The problem seemed to be in the rate of return on my investment of time. I was spending approximately eight hours a week on the phone. Each client was paying $500 -$750 per month for four weekly calls. This was cutting into time that was better spent doing other projects. The financial return just didn't make sense considering the time required to make the calls, prepare, review notes, etc.

I finally came to the conclusion that it was time to take things to the next level. I stepped back from coaching and began focusing all of my energy on developing powerful content for speeches.

It was then that I put pen to paper and created *The Choice Is Yours, Put Your Best Into Action,* and *I Want, I Will, I Win.* My first opportunity to deliver *Choice* came in the summer of 2008 when I was asked to speak for a large group of pharmaceutical reps in Chicago, IL. I was given sixty minutes onstage and a five figure paycheck. This was the perfect event to introduce my new keynote.

The audience was made up of salespeople who worked mainly on commission and were constantly looking for ways to up their game. While backstage, I listened to the CEO of the company deliver the welcoming announcements and lead into my intro video. From where I stood behind the curtain, I could hear the mumbling of recognition. This was good. That sound meant I'd have that instant rapport that is necessary to connect.

During rehearsal earlier that day, I had asked to enter the conference room from the back so I'd have to walk through the crowd to get to the stage. The stage manager took me out and around to back door just as I was being introduced. A spotlight hit me as my intro music kicked in and I came running down the middle of the audience.

Every head turned around as I shook hands and hi five'd as many attendees as I could reach. Every slap of a hand meant another connection and by making my way through the room I had established myself as one of them rather than a figure on the stage. Through my entrance, my choice of words, and my message I had entered their design of the world. Doing so kept them awake, engaged, and receptive to what I had to say.

The Choice Is Yours is more than a speech. It is the result of equal measures education, entertainment, psychology, and blustery showmanship. It is my baby and I've now had the pleasure of delivering it at major conventions, corporate events, universities, civic groups, schools, and churches from coast to coast and sea to shining sea.

Through these live presentations, I was now connecting with hundreds, sometimes thousands, of people in the time I would've spent coaching just one person. And yes...I was making a lot more money.

If you would have asked me in 1990 if I thought I would ever be a life coach, I probably would've responded by asking, "What's a life coach?"

I'm so grateful for the relationships I've formed through my speaking engagements and my work in this field. I'm even more grateful for the things I've learned about myself as a result. Through my experiences with others, I become more patient, more understanding, and more tolerant.

I've worked with so many great achievers and have gained as much from the experiences as my clients have. Sometimes all we need is a fresh set of eyes and a clear perspective to open us up to a new way of thinking. As this chapter now comes to a close, I encourage and challenge you to open your eyes and your mind to the countless possibilities for achievement and fulfillment that are all around you. What are you able to pull from the ashes of that burned down Burger King? Who knows? What you may stumble upon just may be your well deserved ticket to happiness or the next step on your path to greatness.

CHAPTER 9
SPREAD YOUR WINGS AND FLY

I've heard it too many times to ignore it. It's something that I'm supposed to be. Someday we'll find it, the Rainbow Connection. The lovers, the dreamers, and me.
-The Rainbow Connection, Kermit

CONTRARY TO POPULAR OPINION, I do not have a short attention span. I may have thrown in the towel on my restaurant career after only one shift, but I'm actually more guilty of holding on to an idea too long. Not only do I frequently beat a dead horse, but I usually stand there and stare at the corpse until the rotting stench becomes too much for me to handle. The fact that I no longer, except in very rare situations, conduct one on one coaching sessions has nothing to do with quitting or abandoning the mission. As has happened many times in my life, one road simply led to another. It is not in my nature to get involved with something (or someone) unless I plan on seeing it through to the end. It's just that sometimes that ending comes a little sooner than I had expected. When you sink your teeth into a new endeavor you've got to ride it until the wheels fall off. Otherwise you'll be forced to wonder if perhaps you let go a little too soon. Premature desertion is not something I could comfortably live with. Because of this, I feel it is always better to be the last one to leave the party rather than the one who takes off while there are still chips in the bowl.

Failure, as most people define it, is nothing to be ashamed of. Personally, I'm of the school that believes there is no failure, only *feedback*. Even the space shuttle is off course 98% of the time. It reaches its destination by constantly adjusting. Anyone who has ever attended a motivational seminar or read a self help book has heard Thomas Edison's famous quote regarding the invention of the lightbulb. "I have not failed. I've just found 10,000 ways that won't work," said Edison. That's a genius way of thinking from a man who possessed an incredible belief in what he had set out to do. Edison only saw one outcome and, therefore, provides the perfect example of someone who never let go of an idea.

On a visit to the Edison winter estate in Ft. Myers, FL, I learned that Edison holds the world record for patents filed (1,903). In addition to the light bulb and the phonograph, he is responsible for introducing such commercial successes as the talking doll and the alkaline battery. One idea led to another, and another. Edison knew, and you also know, that there is no finish line when it comes to creativity and ambition.

Our thoughts, dreams, and ideas are completely our own and, like you, are completely unique. There may never be another Edison, but there will never be another *you*, either. We may look identical but have different religious beliefs. We may come from the same parents but have different culinary tastes. Look at me and my brother, Jarrod. Same color hair, same upbringing, but opposite personality types. Every man, woman, and child wakes up each morning with a different agenda and all of them work perfectly. None should be labeled broken or wrong. You are who you are and you want what you want. It is what makes you *you*.

*Sharing a laugh with Tom Hanks and Rita Wilson
on the red carpet. 2008.*

The last time I looked, what we are meant to become is not listed on our birth certificates. We are not genetically programmed to develop into doctors, teachers, or game show hosts. I am of two minds when it comes to the "Nature vs. Nurture" debate. Both camps produce some valid points. I've read some fascinating studies on the subject, particularly the *LOGIC* study conducted by the Max Planck Institute for Cognitive and Brain Sciences, and have come to the personal conclusion that we become who we become by little more than good old fashioned trial and error. There's no question Hippocrates would have much to say in rebuttal, but finding out for ourselves what brings us pleasure and what brings us pain undoubtedly leads us to choosing our paths in life. This applies to if we prefer a Mac over a PC, where we choose to live, and what we end up doing to pay the bills.

At the time of this writing, the generation known as "Baby Boomers" is the largest chunk of the American population, totaling approximately 77 million people. The term refers to men and women born between 1946-1964 and, as you can well imagine, a group of this size controls a significant portion of the wealth and spending power in our country. Sadly, economic concerns are causing many of these people, now nearing the age of retirement, to either continue working or rejoin the labor force. Many who fall within this age group are finding themselves being replaced by a younger, cheaper version of themselves or simply seeing their positions eliminated altogether. Rather than lay down and play dead, some have used this as an opportunity to start their own small businesses. Many experts say there has never been a better time to branch out on your own. Big corporations are struggling, startup costs are lower than they have been in years, and customers are looking for a cheaper alternative. According to a 2010 study by the Small Business Administration (SBA), more small businesses are lasting longer than in years past. 51% now survive at least five years. How's that for a kick in the pants? That certainly doesn't guarantee success but, let me remind you that never in the history of mankind has there been such a guarantee.

People venture out into new territory for reasons other than financial necessity. Curiosity, for instance. There are times in your life when an idea turns you on to such a degree that you know deep inside there is no choice but to pursue it and see how it pans out. Every great success story originated as nothing more than an idea. A tiny seed that was planted just to see what it would grow into. Sometimes it amounted to nothing more than a little sprout. But in rare instances, that seed grew into a mighty oak.

How many times have you been in a store and come across an item in aisle 3 that you thought of ten years prior? It has happened to all of us. The fact that I never acted on my hunch to bottle water and sell it haunts me still. When I was a host on Home Shopping Network I was constantly amazed at how many people purchased the most ordinary of items. I once featured a product that was designed to keep your bananas from getting smashed when you brought your lunch to work. It was nothing more than a piece of plastic shaped like a banana (it actually looked like a see-thru marital aid) that came apart in the middle. That was it! You placed the banana inside, threw it in your purse or briefcase, and you were guaranteed a fresh, intact banana when lunchtime rolled around. As I stood in front of the TV camera talking about this item, becoming increasingly self conscious from holding it, I could not believe how quickly the ticker was moving. The ticker is a monitor on a screen that shows the host how many pieces of the item have sold. I'm now convinced that people will pay for *anything* if it is presented in a convincing way. Somebody was making serious money because of an idea that was probably born simply from a mushy banana. I'm curious how many of those shoppers were buying the banana protector to use as it was intended. Hmmmm...

Powerball: Instant Millionaire at the Venetian
in Las Vegas. 2005.

In the game show world, if you take your shoe off and throw it you're bound to hit someone who believes they have the next big show idea. Screenwriters for film are extremely creative people, but they do not hold a candle to the drive that a true gamer possesses when he thinks he's developed the next *Wheel of Fortune*. I come across a lot of these guys, and I only say 'guys' because I've yet to be pitched a new concept by a female. They are often fans who contact me online or attend tapings, producers on their way up, or execs who are looking to add a lucrative CREATED BY credit to their name. Not all of the ideas will make it to the screen, obviously, but it won't be due to a lack of passion on the part of the creator. I am always enamored by their belief and their vision. Whether the show succeeds or it doesn't is not the point. What is important, and what I always point out to them, is that they must believe in their project and follow it through to the very end. Otherwise they will never know for sure and that is much worse than falling short. Imagine going to see *Rocky* and leaving before the end of the Apollo Creed fight. I shudder at the thought.

Sometimes when a television show doesn't make it, it is seen as a failure. Nothing could be further from the truth. It may not be the outcome you hoped for at the outset, but in the process of pursuing your dream you have learned what you should do differently the next time around, you've made valuable contacts, and you've (hopefully) developed a greater confidence in your abilities. These are valuable lessons that you can't learn in school or read online. There is no price tag for such wisdom. It is only found through experience.

Sometimes we have to be knocked down to make us look up. This is quite often when we discover a new direction in which to travel. I believe that many doors fly open after another is slammed shut. Keeping my mind open and my head clear has kept me busy over the years. Even more importantly, it has kept me engaged. Time becomes meaningless when you're engaged in something that genuinely interests you.

For me, MC'ing in nightclubs led to radio. Radio led to TV. TV led to coaching. Coaching led to speaking. And speaking led me someplace I never in a million years could have predicted. Stage hypnotism.

I've touched on the importance of modeling good behavior and positive traits. In NLP, we teach that a person can emulate the practices or behavior of someone who performs well in a certain task or situation in order to better themselves in that same circumstance. A perfect example of this is when a young athlete takes on the characteristics of his or her favorite pro player. Maybe the youngster runs, shoots, catches, or skates in the same fashion as the pro. Perhaps he or she wears the same brand of shoe or does the same touchdown dance. Learning what has worked for someone who has achieved a desirable level of what you are wanting to accomplish yourself can be a vital asset in your success.

In my *America's Life Coach* chapter, I mentioned how Tony Robbins is someone for whom I have great respect. I respect him not only because he has changed millions of lives with his programs, but also because he takes a private jet to work and owns his own island in Fiji. One reason Tony is so effective on stage, and why his seminars never fail to reach standing room only capacity, is because Tony incorporates conversational hypnosis into the presentation. This doesn't mean he puts you into a trance and plants the need to purchase his latest DVD deep into your subconscious. It simply means he uses words, phrases, tonality, and timing to connect with his audience on a more powerful and memorable level.

Some people are visual and need to see something to believe it. Some of us are audible creatures and more taken by the spoken word. There's also a considerable portion of the population that is labeled as kinesthetic. These are the the people who won't buy the sheep until they've felt how soft the wool is. No audience is comprised of only one category. A visual person may tune out if you target the audibles. As communicators, the key for us is to learn how to present in a way that reaches the largest percentage of the group. Thus, we are assured that our presentations will produce the maximum impact. Tony obviously knows what he's doing, so a' modelin' I went.

I purchased countless conversational hypnosis programs and read so many books on the subject that my eyes are still crossed. Mostly I just learned what to say to women to get them to fall for me. That's all fine and dandy, but not exactly what I was looking for. I decided to delve even deeper and study hypnotherapy. Hypnotherapy is becoming a more widely accepted form of therapy and treatment as the years go on. In fact, many states are now covering clinical hypnosis under their insurance programs. I contacted the New England Institute of Hypnotherapy and began my training. Again, because of the amount of time I spend on airplanes and in hotel rooms, I had more time than most to focus on the information. I sailed through the course and, within eighteen months, became a clinical hypnotherapist. After another six month program, and hypnotizing most of my friends for practice, I was an advanced clinical hypnotherapist and had everything I needed to get out there and start putting what I had learned to good use. Not to mention I had become a big hit at cocktail parties.

I worked with individual clients off and on for a few months but never really enjoyed the process. Though it was rewarding to be assisting those who were looking to lose weight or stop smoking, the hours dragged by for me and, like personal coaching, the money wasn't anything to write home about. I once booked a conference room at a small hotel in Providence, RI, and advertised a group hypnotherapy session for anyone looking to make healthier lifestyle choices. My plan was, rather than working with one person for an hour, to conduct a group session of up to thirty people in that same time frame. If I could increase my financial gain thirty times over it would become a little more appealing. As it turns out, only a handful of people showed up. I led the session, sold a few of my CDs, and drove home feeling disappointed. My days as a hypnotherapist were over.

The following week I returned to Las Vegas to host *The Price Is Right Live!* at Ballys. Performing at the casino next door was my friend Anthony Cools. Anthony is a stage hypnotist who enjoys great success in Vegas because his show is downright hysterical. He's such a great guy and always accommodating when I ask to slip in the back of his theater and watch. One night, as I sat in the audience laughing at a woman on stage who had forgotten her own name, it hit me. I could do this! I was fascinated with hypnosis *and* I was a performer. I couldn't believe that I hadn't thought of it sooner. I would become a stage hypnotist and create a show that was different from anything American audiences had ever seen.

Anthony and I had a drink after the show and I told him what I planned to do. He was cool about it (pun intended) and I really respect that. Many performers would have felt like I was stepping on their toes, but that was the furthest thing from my mind. I believe there is plenty of work out there for everyone and have never been one to invade someone else's territory. Cools was generous and supportive. A great entertainer but an even better friend.

I learned a lot from watching Anthony as well as from visiting other shows. While Anthony's show is nonstop laughter, some of the others were just plain awful. Good or bad, one thing had become very clear to me. Although there are no limits to the imagination, there is certainly a limit to the types of routines hypnotists are able to perform. Role playing and acts of amnesia being among the most popular. We have to remain conscious of possible injury to the people who join us on stage. We also have to consider the parameters of the subconscious. If you make a suggestion that takes the subject out of his internal comfort zone he will pop right out of the trance state and you'll be left with nothing. I've been asked on more than one occasion if I'm going to have someone do something awful on stage. The truth of the matter is a hypnotist cannot make someone do anything that goes against that person's moral or ethical code. You're not going to go hold up a gas station with a toothbrush just because a hypnotist tells you to. That is the type of suggestion that would wake anyone right up. The hypnotist needs to set boundaries and adhere to them. A good show is ten percent hypnosis and ninety percent stage savvy. All my years in front of audiences were going to be of great value as I began my journey down this new road.

Hypnosis as a form of entertainment can be a tough sell. One reason for this is there are a lot of people who don't believe it's possible to actually put another person into a trance. Contrary to what we have seen on television and in the movies, hypnotizing someone does not mean turning a poor, unsuspecting woman into a zombie. Hypnosis is simply a deeply relaxed state that actually requires great concentration and awareness on the part of the subject. They do it to themselves. The hypnotist is only the frontman. James "The Amazing" Randi once described hypnosis to me as "an agreement between the subject and the facilitator to fantasize together." I would agree.

Another obstacle that arises when trying to book a show is the question of "what if no one volunteers to come on stage?" Well, that would certainly be awful, but it would never happen. People are not going to buy a ticket to come see a hypnosis show without having some interest in how it all works. That wouldn't make sense. There is not a single person who has ever been in the audience of a hypnosis show who hasn't at least *thought* about going on stage. The curiosity factor is just too high. Many will firmly state that they are not able to be hypnotized. And they would be correct. It is impossible to hypnotize someone who *does not want* to be hypnotized. On the other hand, everyone on the planet can be hypnotized if they *want* to be. Technically speaking, my show begins the very moment people enter the theater. As they take their seats, all they see on the stage is a microphone stand and a row of empty chairs. Instantly, their minds start asking, "What would happen if I got up there tonight?" By the time I finally make my entrance, half the people in the audience have convinced themselves that they are going to volunteer for what could be a once in a lifetime experience. Sure, there's a bit of mind play involved. But that is exactly what has made the mental arts a popular form of live entertainment since the 1800's.

I began stocking my bookshelves with everything I could find on stage hypnotism. I read Ormond McGill's *The Encyclopedia of Stage Hypnotism* not once but twice. That thing is thicker than the Bible but filled with great material. I also read a book called *Deeper and Deeper* by a British hypnotist by the name of Jonathan Chase. I enjoyed Jonathan's style of writing and his techniques for rapid induction. The hypnotic induction refers to the actual process of putting someone into the trance state. The training I had received for hypnotherapy taught inductions that could take as long as thirty minutes. This was much too lengthy for a stage show and I had seen Anthony Cools do it in a fraction of the time. I just had to learn to do it for myself and Jonathan claimed to be one of the fastest.

I read another one of Jonathan's books, *Don't Look In His Eyes*, and knew that he was who I wanted as a mentor. Jonathan runs the Academy of Hypnotic Arts in England and conducts weekend long training seminars a couple of times a year. As great of a teacher as he is, I was looking for something a little more up close and personal. I don't really do well in group learning environments so I sent him an email requesting some individual tutoring. Jon responded by letting me know that he did not ordinarily do that type of teaching but would make an exception in my case if I came to England and agreed to work by his rules. He was feisty and I liked that. We agreed on a fair price for the mentorship and the next thing I knew I was on a plane crossing the pond.

Jon, along with his longtime love and business partner Jane, met me at the airport in Manchester, England, approximately three hours outside of London. Jon is now in a wheelchair which only adds to his mystique. Within five minutes of collecting my bags, he began doing some slight of hand magic and asking some not so slight personal questions. He has deep affection and appreciation for his craft and wanted to make sure I did, as well. That was the first step in deciphering what kind of student I would be. As new as I was to the whole hypnosis scene, I knew I had selected the right teacher and was ready to play the willing student.

We passed the time during the hour long trip through the English countryside with great conversation. As Jon drove us past green pastures filled with dairy cows and old stone houses, we spoke on politics, religion, and our backgrounds. He is a fascinating man who knows how to craft a story. Maybe it's just the fact that he's a legendary hypnotist, but you feel as if he's looking right into your very soul every time he speaks to you.

We finally arrived at the bed and breakfast where I would be staying. Sitting on a cliff high above the English Channel, the tiny B&B was run by a charming retired couple who waited on me hand and foot. The setting was gorgeous. Picturesque landscaping overlooked the water as parrots provided chatter that, at times, was as colorful as their feathers. Jon's home was just a short walk away so I unpacked my bags, took a hot shower to wash away the fatigue from my flight, and made my way down the hill for my first dose of mental arts schooling.

Jon and Jane opened their home to me in every way. For four days we worked from early morning until late at night. I learned all there is to learn about the history of hypnosis, the European style of hypnotism, and how to "drop" a subject into trance within just a few minutes. His methods are amazing and possessed that theatrical, dramatic flair I felt was missing from many of the shows I had seen in America. I was continuously dumbfounded, even while sitting in Jon's living room watching him work on Jane. That feeling of "Wow!" was exactly what I was looking to create with my own show.

Jon and I worked on developing routines that I could bring back to U.S. audiences with me. Together we created a set list that, at least to my knowledge, had never been done before. It was Jon who suggested I incorporate aspects of my television career into my stage show. Although it had been staring me in the face all along, this one element would differentiate me from other hypnotists simply because none of them had my background. Routines like *Hypno Game Show* in which four subjects answered questions while under different suggestions, *Red Carpet* where subjects took on the identities of various celebrities, and *Talk Show* where I put volunteers in different Springer-like scenarios all tapped into my experience as an entertainer and took my performance to a new level. It was off the charts. With my arsenal now fully loaded, it was time to return home and start booking some shows.

The first call I made was to Bill Borenstein, a friend of mine from Atlantic City who was now in charge of entertainment for a large casino in Detroit, MI. Up to this point Bill had only known me as a game show host so you can imagine how shocked he was to hear what I was proposing. I had no demo video, no past show experience, nothing at all to show him what he would be getting, but I knew he would be my best shot. Bill is old school show business and has done deals with some of the biggest names in entertainment. He knew me well enough to know that I could pull off just about anything and we reached an agreement that would allow me to perform in his theater. One night. One show. Do or die. He would help fill the seats by sending out free tickets to his high rollers. It was the break I needed to get me on my way.

Because of the size and the importance of this particular show, I hired another friend of mine to videotape the whole thing for me. The theater in which I would be performing was beautiful and would make for a fabulous sales reel which I would definitely need going forward. No one else was going to pay to have me perform sight unseen.

Wanting this night to be top notch in every aspect, I felt that incorporating a stellar stage assistant was a must. Every performer, whether a magician or a hypnotist, has a beautiful model by his side. The first person that came to mind was Sonja, a woman with whom I'd had a relationship while I was working in Tampa. Sonja is a gorgeous girl and one of the most elegant and sexy runway models I have ever laid my eyes upon. Shortly after being hired at HSN, another male host and I were unofficially asked to stay away from dating any of the models as it could lead to trouble. I was happy to comply until I saw Sonja. Six feet tall, long legs, red hair, and as sweet as she could be. I was fresh from my divorce and utterly defenseless.

Sonja and I were inseparable until my HSN contract expired and my time in Tampa came to an end. She felt abandoned in Tampa and I missed her terribly in Los Angeles. It was a risk to reach out two years later and ask for this favor, but I knew she was the only one for the job. I would have understood if she had simply hung up the phone, but she agreed to be a part of the show. Having her in Detroit would not only allow us to spend a couple of days together, but would also give me the confidence that comes from knowing you're working alongside the very best.

The casino arranged some interviews on local TV and radio to promote our show. There seemed to be a nice interest and tickets were selling well. My parents were flying in to see it and everything was going along smoothly until the day before I was scheduled to leave.

I rarely get sick and when I do it's never more than just a stuffy nose. There's never been anything I couldn't work through, but I could tell this time was going to be different. I woke up that morning with no voice, a raw throat, and a spinning head. My appetite was gone and I couldn't even get out of bed because my body was aching so badly.

I have never once cancelled a show due to sickness, but was feeling as if I may have no other choice. Doing so, however, would cost me $5,000. That was quite the incentive. Fortunately, I was able to sleep off and on for 24 hours and, the next day, somehow found the strength to make it to the airport.

Loaded to the gills with every cold medicine under the sun, I boarded my plane and just waited for my head to explode so I could be put out of my misery. The NyQuil kicked in somewhere over Philadelphia and I slept until we landed in Detroit. Sonja's plane arrived at about the same time and, for the first time in 48 hours, I smiled as I saw her walk through the gate. We held hands as we made our way to the hotel and it felt as if we had never been apart. I'm sure I wasn't great company, but she took care of me the rest of the day and into the night. That evening we had dinner with my parents. Between having my mom and Sonja there, I knew I'd be back to fighting shape in no time.

The morning of the show I was scheduled to do an interview on a local television news program. I wanted to captivate the audience and do something that most hypnotists consider to be the kiss of death...hypnotize someone on live TV. Normally this is a risk that is not worth taking. It is very difficult to put someone into a trance when you're dealing with TV cameras, bright lights, and a lot of strangers meddling around. Most people find it impossible to relax in that kind of environment. If the person you're attempting to hypnotize doesn't go under, you'll look like a fraud and your show will be doomed. Against the advice of many, I asked the PR person from the casino to please find a subject for me. I wanted it to be a total stranger so that there would be no question as to the authenticity of what I was doing. He found a woman named Leigh who was willing to drive in from Kalamazoo to appear with me.

Leigh was perfect. She told me before the program that she had always wanted to be hypnotized and the fact that she drove an hour and a half that early in the morning proved it. We slipped into one of the green rooms so she could mellow out a bit. I asked her if it would be alright if I put her under then and there and she agreed. Leigh was an amazing subject and slipped right into a deep trance. While she was under I gave her the suggestion that the relaxation she was now feeling was only the tip of the iceberg. In fact, the louder things got and the more people that came around, the more relaxed she would become. Bright lights, cameras, and knowing tens of thousands of people were watching would only take her deeper and deeper and make her feel more and more calm. The more I spoke the more her chin fell to her chest. She was mine.

By the time we walked onto the set, I had taken her in and out of trance three times. In truth, a person can be sitting straight up with their eyes wide open and still be hypnotized. But at my command, Leigh would instantly drop into that slumped over position that would come across as very convincing to the people watching at home. It was the visual the audience would expect to see and what I hoped would persuade them to come to the show that night. After a brief interview with the host, I snapped my fingers and gave the command, "Sleep!" Leigh was out like a light. It had worked! We performed a few acts of amnesia that appeared mysterious and dramatic. I could not have asked for anything better. I woke her up and left her feeling as rested and as energized as she would after a four hour nap. It's hard to say how many tickets we sold as a result of that appearance, but I know we made an impact.

As showtime grew closer I began to get a little nervous. People often ask if I ever get the pre-show jitters. The answer is yes and no. I do get butterflies before any performance but it's more of the "*I can't wait to get out there and do this*" variety. The same feeling that makes falling asleep on Christmas Eve virtually impossible. Some friends and members of the press had gathered in my dressing room for a couple of interviews and to wish me well. The mood was light, but their presence made it tough for me to sneak out and see what the house looked like. Taking a little peak at the audience from the side of the stage lets me know what I'll be working with and, every once in a while, gives me a glimpse of a really enthusiastic audience member that I make a note of to use later in the show. I didn't have that luxury in Detroit and I was beginning to feel a bit anxious. At ten minutes before curtain, Bill came in and ushered everyone out to their seats. Sonja went out to take a look for me. Her report back was the place was a little over half full. That was very good news as the theater is rather large. Intimacy plays a big part in a hypnosis show because most of the comedy comes from being able to clearly see the subjects on stage. If someone is sitting too far back the whole show is lost on them.

Everyone sensed that I needed a few minutes alone. I closed the door to my dressing room, sat down on the couch, and put on some slow blues music. I always have a picture of the kids with me when I work. I don't believe in luck, but tonight I was going to need everything I could get so I taped the photo of Mason and Kiki up on the dressing room mirror. Looking at their faces puts my focus right where it needs to be. The reason I was there at all, taking on this new adventure, was for them. I often sit backstage and think about how fortunate I am to be doing what I do for a living. Having the opportunity to entertain people is something I cherish and I always put everything I have into it. Ready or not, here I was...nervous or not, there was no turning back now. Just as I had been doing for weeks, I went through the entire show in my mind one last time as the sounds of Elmore James wailing away played softly in the background.

Jalen, my cameraman, brought me out of my haze by knocking on the door. He wished me luck as he made his way out to where the cameras were stationed. He and I have been working together on live shows for almost ten years and his role in being there was much greater than just capturing some quality video footage. He was, and is, a calming presence. Sonja came out of her dressing room and was a sight for sore eyes in her tight, black dress. She gave me a little kiss before taking her position on the other side of the stage. I was so happy she was there. She would keep me focused and any performer will tell you that there are times on stage when you are just on autopilot. You find yourself drifting off as you recite the lines and going through the motions that you have gone through a million times before. This isn't because we're bored with what we're doing. It happens because we are human and sometimes the brain starts thinking about whatever it is it wants to think about. The performance never suffers because of it and it never lasts long, but it does happen. Tonight was different for me. I wasn't going out on that stage as a speaker or as a game show host. I was going out as a hypnotist. This was completely new territory and I definitely asked myself, "What the hell am I doing?" more than once, but I had done all the prep work I could possibly do and now there was nothing left but to give the audience what they had come to see.

As the lights flashed directing people to take their seats, the fear of no one volunteering popped back into my head. What *would* I do? It would be a disaster. I'd literally crumble in front of my parents, Bill, and Sonja. Word would spread like a California brushfire and my hypnotic career would be over before it even started. I tried as hard as I could to push all negative thoughts from my mind and just focus on the here and now. I didn't have too much time to dwell on it. Without warning, my intro music kicked on and I heard Bill's voice announce me.

"Ladies and gentlemen, please welcome Mr. Hypnotastic...Todd Newton!'

Before I knew it I was on stage in front of 750 people. The thought of being alone in front of an audience of strangers is the number one fear in the world. I've never understood that. Like many fears, I think people conjure up horrible and unrealistic scenarios in their minds when it comes to being the center of attention. As someone who has made a living for over twenty years standing on stages big and small and yelling into a microphone, basically making money for doing what no one else could picture themselves doing, I'm happy to say I've never encountered a hostile audience. Other than the occasional heckler, I've always felt very much at home while on display. I suppose being vulnerable suits me. I feel safe having no one else to rely on other than myself. When I was fifteen years old, I performed standup comedy at open mic nights and would bomb terribly. I don't know if I ever got a single laugh. It's a wonder the audience didn't ask for their money back after realizing they'd paid to watch some kid. But hearing the silence in that smokey club week after week took away all fear because nothing, on any stage in any town, would ever be worse than that. Looking out at all of those smiling Michigan faces ready to be entertained immediately put me at ease and I felt in control. Unlike magic or mentalism, there are no secrets to hypnosis. It's just a bunch of empty chairs, a microphone, and you. What I had asked for had been tossed right into my lap. Now I had to make something of it.

HYPNOSIS Live! begins with my opening monologue. A dramatic foray into the history of hypnotism, it is specifically designed to provide answers to questions the audience may be asking themselves. This is followed by the call for volunteers and an hour's worth of routines which I have the luxury of rearranging as I see fit. Ultimately, it has become a seamless ninety minute performance.

When the time came to ask audience members to push aside their inhibitions and join me on stage, I literally closed my eyes, raised my arms out to the sides like I had seen so many preachers do, and just went for it. Whatever was to happen would happen. Good fortune then fell upon me right there in the Motor City. Normally, ten to fifteen subjects is what you hope for. On this given night, no fewer than forty volunteers joined us onstage to be a part of my first show. In fact, there were so many willing souls that we ran out of chairs and many were left standing. It was quite a spectacle! I looked over at Sonja and she gave me a reassuring smile. The audience and I were working in perfect harmony with each other. With the nervousness now a thing of the past, it was time to just have some fun.

*Performing my stage hypnosis show at the
Motor City Casino in Detroit. 2010.*

An hour and a half flies by when you're really in the zone and before I knew it, it was time to bring it all home. Casinos want shows to stick to a tight ninety minutes so the guests can get back out onto the floor and hit the gambling tables. With only fifteen minutes remaining, I realized I had to abandon a few bits and proceed right into my finale. For a closer, I needed something the audience would be laughing about well after the show was over. The *Vibrating Chair* is a variation of the popular *Handshake Orgasm* done by many hypnotists. No one, however, does it better than Anthony Cools. I have never "worked blue"-performed bawdy material-so I went with the family friendly version of the bit. One by one, I called each volunteer out to a chair Sonja had placed at center stage. I thanked them for participating in the show then shook their hand. As a result of the suggestion I had previously given, as soon as I took their hand in mine they would immediately feel an incredible tingling sensation that started at the top of their head and shot down to the tips of their toes. The longer I shook the more intense the feeling would become and they would *love* it! I didn't need to spell it out. The audience knew exactly what I was up to and the bit worked like a charm. The guests on stage were laughing hysterically as if they were being tickled and the crowd was rolling in the aisles. It was the perfect ending to the perfect show. I threw up a piece sign and held it long enough for my cameraman to capture it before exiting stage right. Sonja was right there waiting. With sweat pouring off of my body, I thanked the backstage crew for a job well done and made my way to the dressing room. The cold bottle of Heineken that was waiting for me could not have tasted better.

As part of my contract, I was required to appear at a short reception for the casino's VIP's. I never mind these types of obligations. Meeting people is what it's all about and this was an interesting group of big gamblers, important clients, and friends of the executives. When you spend most of your professional life speaking into the lens of a camera you sometimes forget that people actually watch what you're making. A nice meet & greet puts you face to face with the audience that is keeping the home fires burning. I was especially excited to meet this audience because I was craving feedback in a big way. If the show wasn't as entertaining as it had felt to me then I wanted to know so I could make changes. The only way to grow is to receive and accept criticism...good or bad. Everyone I spoke to, however, was very complementary.

After the photos and the thank you's, I made my way to the lobby to find my parents. Several friends had made the trip from St. Louis and congratulated me on the show. There were even a couple of local hypnotists and some game show fans that had hung around to say hello. My satisfaction grew with every compliment. I am my own worst critic and knew of several things I would do differently in the next performance, but overall it was a wonderful night and most certainly a hell of a first time out. But, as we all know, life is all about peaks and valleys.

If that first show was perfect, then my next hypnosis gig must be labeled as anything but. In October of 2010, I traveled to Egypt to speak and conduct a hypnosis event on the Nile River. I returned home in time to go trick or treating with my kids on Halloween and was contacted by a local publicist about booking a show in the Boston area. I had never performed for the local crowd and it seemed like a fun idea. He explained that he had a small venue south of the city that would provide the perfect environment. It was a hip jazz club that did good business. There had never been a hypnosis show in the area and he was confident the turn out would be huge. I was becoming more and more involved with Soles4Souls and offered to wave my performance fee if a portion of the cover charge could be donated to the organization in order to send shoes over to Haiti. He agreed and a we set the show for early December.

With the date well over a month away, I went off to Europe for a series of speaking engagements and left the publicity solely in his hands. Producing events is was what he did for a living so I figured our small one-nighter was pretty much a slam dunk. My first mistake was assuming all the bases would be covered and not checking in on how things were being handled. My second mistake was agreeing to do a show in Boston in the middle of winter.

The snow was falling faster than the temperature on the day of the show. I called the booker and expressed my concern about attendance but he assured me that people would turn out. He was either dreaming, lying, or both. When I arrived at the club that evening the parking lot was desolate. If it wasn't for the Pizza Hut next door there wouldn't have been any signs of life on the entire block.

Things only got worse when I walked inside. The place was a dump. I mean, even the dumpiest dumps would call this joint a dump. The stage barely had room for me and three chairs. I should've asked what his definition of 'hip' was because clearly it was different from mine. When I picture a jazz club, I envision plush, red furniture under dimly lit chandeliers and a funky trio in the corner playing Coltrane and Miles Davis classics. This place was decorated with neon beer signs and wooden barstools. The jukebox gave patrons a choice between Pink Floyd's *The Wall* and INXS' *Greatest* Hits. I personally own both of those albums, but they ain't no Thelonious Monk. Pulling a gig off in this hole in the wall was going to require every trick in the book.

Slowly, people started arriving. They'd stumble through the door, complaining about the cold, and take a seat at the bar to watch the Bruins game. By showtime there were about twenty five people in the place. Half of them were already drunk and the other half only stopped in to shoot pool or throw darts. No one was interested in a hypnosis show. I had worked a lot of dingy clubs in my early days but this one might have been the worst. Canceling the gig and going home began to seem like a really good idea.

In the world of show business, you encounter two types of performers: Those who work only for the paycheck, and those who work to provide the audience with a little bit of entertainment *and* for the paycheck. I guess I fall into the second category. Maybe I was wishing upon a star, but there seemed to be a couple of people out there who came for the show and disappointing them would have kept me up at night. Besides, as drunk and obnoxious as that crowd was, they had contributed to Soles4Souls just by showing up. The least I could do was give them something to talk about for a little while. If I was going to continue calling myself a pro, then it was time to pull up my trousers and step up to the plate.

I took the stage with no introduction but with the confidence of a man playing Madison Square Garden. I didn't care how many people had their backs to me or how loud *Sportscenter* was playing on the TV over the bar, someone was getting hypnotized that night. After waiting for the squealing feedback from the microphone to subside, I told them who I was, why I was there, and asked for volunteers to come to the stage.

After some hesitation and debate, four people finally said "What the hell," and came up. Two of them were blitzed beyond belief. They offered nothing I could work with so I immediately dismissed them back to their seats. Another was a young woman who seemed curious enough to give it a whirl. Finally, I came to the final chair on the stage and face to face with a volunteer I somehow hadn't noticed before.. This individual was a gift from hypno heaven-if such a place actually exists. Sitting before me on stage, grinning from ear to ear, was a sixty year old transvestite.

I couldn't have ordered anything more perfect if I'd had the JC Penney catalog at my disposal. Here was a blue collar guy from south Boston who, for reasons only known to him, enjoyed dressing up as a woman. I couldn't believe my luck. Physically speaking, he/she was the ugliest thing you've ever seen, but for what I needed at the moment this person was pure beauty. A short, grey wig hanging crooked off his head. Drugstore makeup apparently applied in the dark. A dress salvaged from a dead aunt's closet. This fella didn't go halfway or pull any punches with his commitment to the cause. Here he/she was. Love it or leave it. The patrons, who minutes before had shown no interest in what I was doing, now could not take their eyes away from the stage. This neighborhood crowd had never seen anything like this. Suddenly I had a captive audience. It was time to turn it on.

The stage was so small that I couldn't even make room for the woman I had brought as my assistant. Quite frankly, with a crowd this size there was no need for her to even be there so she sat off to the side and laughed hysterically. She knew, as did I, that if I could put this senior drag queen *under* (a hypno term meaning into a trance) I would not only salvage this show, but somehow manage to make it one for the history books.

Needless to say, performing with a transvestite presents a couple of professional challenges. This is especially true when the opportunity to do so comes out of nowhere. I mean, if I'd had a little advance notice maybe I wouldn't have stood there so dumbfounded when I realized what I had been given to work with. But this business is all about rolling with the punches.

The first challenge is avoiding the all to easy trap of going for the lowest common denominator in terms of jokes. A solid host/entertainer needs to have a filter when it comes to the things you say-and choose *not* to say-on stage. Our first inclination is to do whatever it takes to please the audience. Their laughter is our drug and it is extremely hard for us to resist. Some performers work with the "sacrifice one for the merriment of many" philosophy, but you only need to feel the sting of crossing the line once to realize it is often better to play it safe. The last thing you ever want to do is offend or hurt someone and I believe I have found a nice middle ground in my performance style. *Entertainment Weekly* once described me as "Smooth and Personable." I take that as a great compliment and attribute it, in part, to the influence Johnny Carson had on me early on. On *The Tonight Show with Johnny* Carson, he became the master of looking straight into the camera and giving the audience watching at home a look that was worth a thousand words. We felt he was looking only at us. Many times he would knock it out of the park while interviewing Dolly Parton or Angie Dickinson without having to say a single word. We knew exactly what he was thinking-and usually it was what *we* were thinking, as well-but he never risked offending the guest with an off color comment or jab. I believe that is what made Johnny so endearing to so many for so long. Bob Eubanks of *The Newlywed Game* was also very good at this. I believe there are some hosts that the audience expects to hear a certain type of remark from. For example, when I'm hosting *The Price Is Right Live!* in a casino and a beautiful woman in a tight shirt is jumping up and down on the stage, everyone in attendance has a pretty good idea of what is going through my mind. I never resort to using dirty material, but I'm also not going to convince anyone that I'm a choirboy. To *not* address this woman (and her choice of attire) would appear unnatural. A simple, well timed look can do the trick nicely, provide a huge laugh, and no one ever gets put off.

I had no way of knowing what kind of life this man in Boston had during a normal day, but I would guess he/she probably gets his/her share of stares and sly comments. You'd have to have a pretty thick skin to walk around Beantown making that kind of statement. In a way, I guess it's admirable. Regardless, I don't judge others and had no intention of adding to any strain he may encounter. He/she was there to have fun and so was I.

The second challenge that comes from working with a cross dresser is that of maintaining stage balance. He/she (and I use this term not in an attempt to be funny, but because his/her name has escaped me) could very easily outshine the other person on stage. Focusing on just one participant can make things seem out of whack. The other volunteer may subconsciously realize they haven't been utilized in a routine in a while and come out of trance, leaving you looking like an amateur. It is key, in any kind of performance, to utilize all that you have been given. Bob Barker taught me to find the gold in every contestant I work with on a game show. The same is also true for volunteers in my hypnosis show, people that I work with in my keynote presentations, and those we encounter in daily life. Everyone has their own story and if you look hard enough you can find it and make it shine. Why carry the whole performance on one or two sets of shoulders when there are others around to help with the heavy lifting? I needed to be wary of becoming all consumed with this unique situation I had found myself in.

Normally, asking the audience for complete silence during the induction process is not a big deal. They are there because they want to see you do what you do so they are going to make it as easy for you as possible. No one buys a ticket to watch a flop. This little dive, however, had all the potential for disaster. The men were there to watch sports. The women were there for the cheap drinks. Being politely quiet wasn't on the menu. Thankfully, the crowd was now all eyes and ears. They were mesmerized. TV's and the jukebox had been powered off and the only sounds heard were the occasional hacking of one of the many chain smokers in attendance and the sticking of my boots to the beer soaked floors. The induction was underway. Within three minutes, my subjects were in one of the deepest trances I've ever been witness to.

I followed up with a couple of deepeners. These are routines designed to take the subjects into an even deeper state of relaxation. I told them to imagine large balloons tied to their wrists and their arms flew up into the air. I told them to imagine watching a funny movie and they began laughing so hard they had tears in their eyes. I told them they had just purchased their dream car and found themselves next to their boss at a red light. Both of them flipped their middle fingers. It was a natural reaction and it was hilarious. The show was heating up and it was time to break out the good stuff.

I tapped into my TV career and did my *Red Carpet* bit. When I asked the tranny who she was, she responded, "John Wayne." The crowd lost it! Here was an over the hill drag queen, in full costume, doing a dead on impersonation of The Duke. The lip was curled up, he/she swaggered across the stage, and even called me 'Pilgrim." Sheer brilliance! I moved on to some amnesia and had him/her forget the number that comes after one and before three. Every hypnotist in the world does this routine and asks a female volunteer to count her breasts in an effort to remember the number, but none of them had *my* female volunteer. He/she cupped each boob while counting out, *"One,...three."* Then he looked right me. I sensed what was coming and put the microphone up to his/her mouth.

"Hmmm. Well, I guess somebody's getting even luckier than he thought tonight," he/she said.

That was it! The punchline of all punchlines and the closer of all closers. I'd only been on for thirty minutes but wasn't about to press my luck any further. I woke my two volunteers up and said my thank you's while the audience was still laughing. My assistant and I got out of there as quickly as we could and drove back to my place feeling as if we'd just pulled off someone's definition of a miracle.

It takes a while for the adrenaline that comes from performing to work through your system, so many times I'll be up later than usual after a show. On this particular night, I immediately went online and sent an email to Jon Chase over in the United Kingdom. I told him about all of the the challenges I'd been presented with, my dream volunteer, the reluctant audience, etc. I was curious if he'd had similar experiences and how he may have dealt with them. Shortly after hitting the Send button, my head hit the pillow. I awoke the next morning to Jon's response waiting for me...

"Congratulations. *Now* you are a hypnotist."

Please don't do yourself the disservice of going through life with blinders on. Don't choose to take the shortest or the safest route when it comes to career, romance, or family. Don't allow yourself to see the unknown as something that should be feared. Don't lose the curiosity we all have as children. Accept each new day with the confidence and strength of knowing that falling on your face really doesn't hurt all that much. Explore new ideas and opportunities, fully accepting whatever may come from them. I promise you it will either be a great success or a beneficial experience. No failure.

There is also no shame in moving *on* as long as you are moving *forward.* If you honestly feel you have reached the end of one road, begin a journey down another. I challenge you today to take one considerable step toward where you want to be. Send a resume, make a call, set up a meeting. Move ahead, attempt something new, create momentum, and go plant the seed that is your idea. Refuse to accept anything resembling a limitation. Come on, the world is waiting for you to spread your beautiful, multicolored wings and fly.

CHAPTER 10
A JOURNEY TO HAITI

From each according to his ability,
to each according to his need.
-Karl Marx

"JESUS CHRIST. I WASN'T expecting this."

Those were my exact words to my friend Wayne Elsey, founder and CEO of Soles4Souls, as we walked through one of many tent cities in Port Au Prince, Haiti, in January of 2012.

The earthquake that struck Haiti on Tuesday, January 12, 2010, at 4:53pm registered a 7.3 and was the largest to hit the area in hundreds of years. The fifty nine aftershocks only added to the physical and emotional devastation. Like Hurricane Katrina in the United States, some experts had warned of the possible disaster but no precautions were taken. That, of course, is not the fault of the citizens who lost everything as a result. It's no one's fault. It's just life. Two years later, life hasn't gotten much better and it sure as hell hasn't gotten any easier.

Wayne founded Soles4Souls in 2004 after watching television news coverage of the Asian tsunami. One shot of a lone shoe that had washed upon the shore caught his attention and instantly he dedicated his life to collecting and distributing footwear to the needy around the world. As of this writing, over seventeen million pairs of shoes have been placed on the feet of those who need them most.

I became aware of Soles4Souls in August of 2010, after reading an article about Wayne in *Success* Magazine. At the time, I was hosting and producing a radio show called *Life Radio with Todd Newton*, and invited him to be a guest. You don't have to spend much time with this man to realize his enthusiasm is contagious. I offered to lend my support to the organization in any way he would see fit. Six months later, I traveled to S4S headquarters in Nashville and committed to being their national spokesperson.

Haiti, and all of its suffering, is closer to home than many Americans realize. Located 750 miles off the coast of Florida, Haiti is Indian for *mountains* and it makes up one third of the island of Hispaniola, which it shares with the Dominican Republic. I wanted to visit Haiti because I felt it was my obligation to witness firsthand what so many have only read about. I assure you the stories you've heard have not been exaggerated. If anything, they have been unintentionally downplayed due to a lack of words that accurately describe the reality.

When Wayne, my friend/cameraman Dan Duffy, and I stepped off our American Airlines flight from Miami, I noticed one characteristic of the Haitian people right away. No one seemed to be asking for a handout. All they wanted was an opportunity. An opportunity to carry my bags. An opportunity to load them into our truck. An opportunity to usher us through the crowded arrivals area. As Americans, we often turn a blind eye and a deaf ear to those who we assume are looking for tips. Blame it on too many nights in the big city, but I must admit that is how I felt at first. I was quickly made to feel otherwise by their smiles and their demeanor. There seemed to be an inner light that was shining in the eyes of each person I met. A light that, in spite of their economical or living situations, did not seem to fade.

After loading and locking our gear in the caged bed of the Kia pickup truck that would be our transportation for the trip, we met a woman who I would soon come to see as an angel. Her name is Anny. Anny would be our guide, our chauffeur, our interpreter, and our big sister on this mission.

Born and raised in Haiti, Anny moved to California shortly after meeting her husband, John. While in CA they had three boys who are now all in their teens. After the earthquake, Anny felt her homeland calling her back and she returned to be of service. Her husband and sons supported her decision and the five of them made the journey as a family. They sold their ranch style home in America and relocated to a studio apartment in Port au Prince. Since then, they have dedicated their professional lives to making a difference with Soles4Souls. Words like generous and charitable do not even begin to describe this beautiful family.

The sun was setting as we made our way across the still busy and bumpy roads to Le Plaza Hotel. As is the case in many smaller, less civilized countries, the streets were packed with cars, trucks, and pedestrians of all ages in an organized scramble. As our truck began to putter to a stop, I swallowed the fumes and dust coming in through my window as I looked for something resembling a hotel. All that was visible to me was a giant, concrete wall. Slowly, a solid eight foot tall gate rattled open from left to right. As we pulled inside I noticed rows of circular barbed wire on top of the walls and armed men in uniform smoking and sweating inside a tiny, wooden guard shack. This definitely wasn't the Four Seasons. We checked into our rooms and agreed to meet in the hotel bar shortly to unwind from our day of travel and discuss tomorrow's itinerary.

My room was not much different from a thousand other hotels that I have stayed in over the years. But it wasn't until the next day that I would come to realize that, to the people struggling to survive just on the other side of that wall, this king sized bed and that hot shower would be like living in Bel Air. I had just enough time for a quick shower before meeting the guys for a Presidente beer or three. As the warm water spit down upon my body, I focused on gratitude...an emotion I channel frequently but which seemed to have a different meaning on this particular evening given my surroundings. After a nice dinner, I returned to my room and quickly fell fast asleep to the gentle humming of the air conditioner.

The following morning I woke up just in time to grab a bite in the same restaurant we'd had dinner in the night before. I love a breakfast buffet. For some reason the eggs just seem to taste better when I know there is an endless supply of them just behind the swinging doors to the kitchen. The coffee was unbelievably delicious and I must have downed a gallon of freshly squeezed orange juice. Who says food on the road is torture?

With our stomachs full, we connected with our security guard, Franz, and proceeded through the large gate of our hotel. We did not anticipate any problems, but decided it would be best to have Franz with us, in full uniform, as we stepped out onto the busy sidewalk and into another world. There were cars and vans honking and zooming by. Children running. People yelling. This was daily life in Haiti and it took me a minute or two to adjust to my surroundings. I stuck close to Franz as we crossed the street and walked toward the tent city. Driving past this area the night before I could only make out the outlines of the tents. Very few had any electricity at all and the dim lighting made it impossible to see what was now impossible to miss. Today, with the light of the sun, I could see the reality.

It is estimated that the earthquake left nearly 800,000 Haitians homeless. The government stepped up and provided "temporary" housing by turning large parks into these tent cities. This particular location was now home to over 100,000 people. Many families cram five or more people into a single room. It was obvious by more than just the smell that a sanitation system was non existent. Trash was everywhere. Partially filled buckets of filthy, brown water served as both bathtubs and laundry facilities. Faces of little children peered out at us from behind dirty sheets in doorways as we passed through. Mothers took a break from hanging clothes out to dry to stare. I wondered what they were thinking. What did they see when they looked at me? It didn't take long for me to find out.

"Hey," shouted a young man of about twenty five.

He was sitting on some concrete steps with a group of women. He rose and began walking through the puddles in the pavement towards me. Franz stepped in between us but I put my hand on his shoulder and said it was alright. I wanted to speak with him. He introduced himself as Lawrence and I was relieved to find that he spoke perfect English. Creole, along with French, is recognized as Haiti's native language, but Lawrence had clearly had some schooling somewhere along the line. I offered my hand as a gesture of friendship and he took it.

Lawrence asked what we were up to and I explained that we were filming a video that would be shown to schools and organizations in America promoting donations of shoes, clothing, and money specifically for Haiti. His response saddened me. Lawrence told me of all the other rescue and charitable organizations that had come through and made promises that had never been kept. Simple promises. School supplies. All they wanted was paper, pencils, glue, and crayons for the young children but no one had come through for him. It was clear he was not a violent man, very few Haitians seemed to be, but hearing the disappointment in his voice leveled me as easy as any punch to the stomach would have. What could I say? There was nothing I could possibly tell him that he hadn't heard before. No matter what I said, he was going to think that I was just another mainlander passing through so I could return home and tell all of my friends what a giving soul I was for visiting a third world country. All I could do was hope that Lawrence would see something in my eyes or hear something in my voice that he could take to heart. Not that I was there to try to wake him up from the nightmare his family and neighbors had been living, but rather that there are people thousands of miles away that actually care. I wanted him to know that there are some of us who lay awake at night thinking about those who are suffering and actually want to go out and do something about it. We talked a little more. Actually Lawrence talked and I just listened. The conversation concluded with another handshake. In a rare occurrence, I was left standing alone with nothing to say.

My exchange with Lawrence stayed with me as we drove to meet a group of extraordinary volunteers who had raised money (or dipped into their own pockets) to join us on this shoe distribution trip. The youngest of them was in her early twenties, the oldest was eighty seven, and they came from all walks of life. Kindness knows no age or race.

One of the most enthusiastic team members was a gentleman named Scott who was on his second trip to Haiti. He had personally raised $30,000 and was excited to see firsthand where that money went. After a quick lunch of djon-djon (pronounced *Jon-Jon* and consisting of rice, beans, and mushrooms), the team loaded onto their bus and led the way to an orphanage where the plan was to distribute soccer balls to the children.

The trip took us an hour over steep, poorly paved roads and past more tent cities, more roadside shacks selling everything from car batteries to live chickens, and through a mass gravesite that brought a moment of silence from everyone in the truck. Upon arriving at the orphanage I realized, once again, that my expectations were completely off base. What do you picture when you imagine an orphanage? A multi-story brick building with a rolling lawn and a sign out front? Maybe a playground on the side? That was what I had in my head, but what stood before me was completely different. The tops of four white tents peaked at us from over another large wall. Upon closer inspection I saw that three of them were crammed with bunk beds. The fourth tent served as a combination cafeteria/classroom. In the corner of the small lot was a metal shack, about the size of the storage shed I once had in my backyard, that served as the community bathroom.

At the orphanage in Haiti with Soles4Souls. 2012.

I heard the kids before I could see them. There is nothing like the joyous shriek of a child and there were plenty of them heading our way. It was like watching children running down the stairs on Christmas morning. They knew our arrival meant new toys and judging by the smiles on their faces, we had perceived their situation to be much worse than they did. They had no intention of letting us stand there and feel sorry for them. We had soccer balls and they were ready to play. I retreated to a corner section of the yard and was soon joined by a group of young boys that seemed to be the same age as my son. Of course, when I say yard I think of the grassy yard I had as a kid. The only obstacle we had to contend with back then was staying out of my mother's flower garden. Here we had to keep from tripping over large rocks and falling on the hard, packed dirt.

We played and played. I'm happy to say that my kickball skills are still sharp after all these years. Soon we were all dripping with sweat. My Soles4Souls t-shirt was like a wet dishtowel stuck to my skin. I rolled up the sleeves in an effort to cool off a little. As soon as I did I was immediately surrounded! The kids had immediately noticed my tattoos and become fascinated by the many shapes, colors, and words. They stood and stared at them as if gazing at the Mona Lisa. Amazed, they slowly reached out to gently touch them as if the ink might somehow smear off. I saw this as an opportunity to bond and taught them the words *tat-too* and *star*. I watched as they giggled amongst themselves and rolled their own sleeves up to expose skinny little biceps. Anny had mentioned earlier that a teacher in Haiti makes approximately $100 a month. I cringed at the realization that the price of just one of my sessions at the tattoo parlor is the equivalent of half a year of employment. Just goes to show you how much we (I) take for granted.

Like all things that children are taken with, the excitement of my body art was soon replaced by some new attraction. Bubble gum, perhaps. But one little boy stuck around. His name was Rafael and, from what I recalled from 9th grade French class, I was able to discern that he was twelve years old. Rafael and I kicked the ball back and forth, played some "keep away," and looked at pictures on my iPhone. I showed him photos of Kiki and some of Mason in his hockey uniform. I'm pretty sure these were among the first pictures of American kids at play that Rafael had ever seen. His interest in my children made me smile. The pure, unbridled, and untainted curiosity of a child really is something to behold. So much so that I occasionally close my eyes and meditate on simply being present. I offer a rebirth to my own wonderment in hopes of rediscovering some of the great beauty that is all around yet, all too often, goes unnoticed. I think that is the main reason I always choose to live by the ocean, whether it be in Marina del Rey, CA, or Boston's south shore, there is just something so peaceful that comes from looking out at the blue water while the rest of the world drifts away. Allowing yourself to just be in the moment. What is life other than a series of moments strung together?

Rafael wore me out. I was tired and sweat had drenched me right down to my Calvin Klein boxer briefs, but I still wasn't ready for our time together to end. I was really enjoying myself and knew that leaving those kids was going to rip my heart out. It did. When the time came for us to load up the truck and head out I found it difficult to climb into the cab. I knew that I had much more to see and do in Haiti but these children would be staying behind. I wanted so badly to bring them with us and show them parts of their own country that they had never seen. I also felt the great need to show them the world that existed outside the walls of that orphanage. A world they may very well never get to experience. I wanted them to know what it was like to ride a roller coaster or experience ordering room service in a nice hotel. I wanted them wake up on Christmas morning and unwrap present after present. I wanted them to just be kids. Apparently I wasn't the only one who was moved by the experience because we drove to our next destination in complete silence. Finally I came to the conclusion that, in spite of the cards life had dealt them, those kids were innately happy. They saw their lives as being just fine and dandy and, as we all know, perception is reality. I found some solace in that as I recalled Rafael's face when I was leaving. He smiled and gave me a wave...and he had barely broken a sweat.

Our next stop was a community center outside of Port Au Prince that had suffered serious structural damage to the roof and foundation as a result of the earthquake. Soles4Souls has committed to rebuilding the roof and assisting the owner with establishing classes and programs for the public. These include occupational training, HIV/AIDS education and screening, dental screening, and recreational programs.

Two key events took place as soon as we pulled into the parking lot. The first of these events, and the one that is certainly less significant but very funny, is our cameraman Dan stepped in a huge pile of fresh, steaming hot dog crap. The second occurred as Dan was scraping the soles of his shoes clean with a pencil, I finally got to meet the man named Dr. Paul.

Dr. Paul is a dentist by trade but a humanitarian at heart. He has taken it upon himself to oversee all that needs to be done to get the center back where it needs to be in order to once again become a safe and happy place for the community. He took me on a tour and shared his grand plan for the place with each step we took. This guy can really talk. I tend to speak quickly, loudly, and a little too closely for the comfort of many, but this guy put me to shame. His enthusiasm almost wore me out as much as playing with Rafael did. He spoke a mile a minute because he had so much to share.

One of Dr. Paul's visions is to host an international basketball tournament at the center. As we walked across the chipped and warped parquet floor, he told me how he dreams of inviting teams from neighboring countries over to Haiti to play. He is convinced that if people would just visit Haiti they would see that it is much more than what is shown on CNN. I believe he's right. He also talked of putting in a portable stage so the staff and the community can produce and enjoy concerts and plays.

This wonderful man then showed me the swimming pool that, as of now, is nothing more than an eight foot concrete tub holding sewer water, but could one day be a refuge from the heat as children laughed, splashed, and learned how to swim. He led me into classrooms that he hopes will soon be filled with computers and other supplies so the people of the surrounding area could learn skills that would empower and enrich their lives. Attendance in one or more scheduled courses per quarter would be all that is required for full use of the community center. Of all the plans that he spoke of, he feels the strongest about providing HIV education AND counseling. Although there has been a decline in HIV cases in Haiti over the past few years, it is still prevalent. Most cases are contracted through heterosexual activity, followed by mother-to-infant transfers.

Education has certainly encouraged prevention and we have seen positive results, but we cannot stop with just education. We must consider those who are diagnosed with the disease and provide them with counseling on how to deal with the new direction their lives are now going to take. Dr. Paul and Soles4Souls have done the research and have the counselors and doctors standing by. All that is needed is the funding. The elusive dollar. If only Dr. Paul could appear on a game show and win a million bucks. Think of the good that would come of that. Dr. Paul remains positive and focused. In America his entrepreneurial spirit would probably shoot him up the ranks of just about any Fortune 500 company, but he isn't about all that. He wants his drive to produce results for others. Not for himself. And I think that is pretty special.

On our final day in Haiti, the team and I went to do what Soles4Souls does best. I finally got to take part in one of their shoe distributions.

As I mentioned earlier, the organization offers several opportunities each year for individuals to raise money and take part in one of these trips. They visit Tanzania, Costa Rica, Peru, Dominican Republic, and, of course, here in Haiti. Many people on this particular trip were there for the "once in a lifetime" aspect it provides and I'm sure it was an experience none of them will forget. The goal is for each attendee to go home and share the story with others, thus raising awareness of the need as well as the effort. Others, like Scott, had been on one, two, even three trips prior to Haiti. I quickly spotted the Travel Coordinator, Emily, and asked her how I could help. She told me just to jump in.

The villagers were lined up out the door. It reminded me of a busy Saturday afternoon at a theme park. It was a *long* line. Upon reaching the entrance to the small, concrete room with little or no ventilation, the man, woman, or child would have their foot measured. Their shoe size would be written on their hand and then they were shown to one of four stations we had set up. There they would meet a smiling volunteer who would be waiting with a tub of water. We'd wash their feet and bring them a pair of shoes. If possible, we'd let them choose between a couple of different pairs. Choices are always good and after a selection was made we'd assist them in slipping the new shoes on and off they would go.

I have an aversion to feet. Other than my children's cute baby toes and a few select women I've known who have had *incredible* feet, they make me gag. Men's feet especially. I feel as if I should devote an entire chapter to why it should be mandatory for men to get regular pedicures and ban open toe sandals, but the subject matter is just too revolting. On this particular day, however, purpose seemed to outweigh revulsion and I washed foot after foot. Big, small, smooth, or calloused I washed those feet like there was no tomorrow. I didn't do a rush job either. I took my time, made sure all the dirt was off, and even gave a good drying to each customer that came my way. When the feet had been cleansed to my satisfaction then, and only then, would the shoes come out.

The boys received sneakers from Under Armor who had made a generous donation. The ladies of Haiti generally prefer slip ons with a short heel. Just goes to show you that a woman wants to look good no matter where she is or what she is doing. We were happy to oblige if we could.

A S4S shoe distribution is a well oiled machine designed to provide as many people with shoes in the most orderly fashion possible. What I had not taken into consideration was the fact that there were undoubtedly going to be more people in line than available shoes. When the shoes are gone they are gone until the next time we come to town. People who have been standing in line under the blazing sun for over two hours want shoes and aren't too thrilled when they find out the party is over. The team, however, was prepared for such a reaction. When the supply was gone, we closed the door for several minutes to give the initial indication that we were finished. This was enough for some of the villagers to see it was time to pull out...but not all.

Preparing this young girl's feet for a much needed new pair of shoes. Haiti, 2012.

Slowly but surely volunteers would exit the room two or three at a time and start making their way back to the bus. Wayne and I stayed behind because I had committed to witnessing the process from beginning to end. I already felt a little strange because we had our own security guard. Being the first one to leave, I felt, would be an arrogant move and not one I was comfortable in making.

With only a handful of volunteers remaining, we began carrying out the empty boxes and loading them on the truck. This made it clear to those still clinging to the hope of a new pair of kicks that Elvis had truly left the building. There was some hustling and bustling-maybe even a curse word or two thrown out in Creole-but overall it went smoothly.

As we drove away I experienced the same emotion I had earlier when leaving the orphanage. It's a feeling that is hard to accurately describe but it's as if we were leaving a job undone. Instead of focusing on we had accomplished-giving all those people new shoes, lowering their risk of contracting disease, putting smiles on the children's faces, etc.-all I could think about was the group of people who did not receive anything that day. Was this just another disappointment in a lifetime of letdowns or was there a chance they knew we would be back soon to take care of them? I suppose it is that realization of work still needed to be done that drives the philanthropic spirit and keeps humanitarianism alive. Maybe...but it didn't make it any easier at the time.

The trip thus far had been exhilarating, rewarding, heart wrenching, and exhausting all at once. I had only been in Haiti for a few days but knew I would be returning before long. For now, though, I was happy to know I'd soon be back home with my kids and sharing all I had learned and seen with them.

On our final night, we had dinner at a lovely restaurant in Port Au Prince. Anny parked the truck and we walked past a group of teenage boys selling iPhone chargers and cases before being seated at our table. Dr. Paul and his wife arrived shortly after we did and said that a friend would be joining us, as well. He was a writer and worked for the Department of Tourism in Haiti. I always like meeting interesting people, especially artsy, creative types, and looked forward to his arrival.

Yves Gerard Olivier, it turns out, is much more than an artsy, creative type. He's a brilliant human being that fascinated me from the moment he sat down. Yves (pronounced *ee-VAY*) had recently written and self published a book recounting the stories of over one hundred fifty earthquake survivors. Amazingly, he had done all of this while living in his car after being left homeless himself. The kicker of it all, and what made me realize for certain that Yves was a special soul, was that he told me he was living in his car with *a smile on his face*. He was just happy to be alive and to be at dinner with other conversationalists. He was thrilled to be making new friends and to have the opportunity to share the passion behind his writing. As someone who normally avoids dinner parties, I'm sure glad I attended this one.

Everyone at our long table, and even some seated at tables nearby, became mesmerized by Yves' telling of the interviews he'd conducted. These were authentic stories of survival and determination, the likes of which I'd never been exposed to before. I'd visited New Orleans shortly after Hurricane Katrina and met with people who had lost it all. I even had lunch with a family who had camped out on their roof with their dog while watching all of their worldly belongings float down the street. I'd also been in New York just weeks after 9/11 and spoken with a widow of a NY fireman who gave his life while trying to save those who were trapped inside what remained of the World Trade Center.

Tales such as these are real life demonstrations of the human spirit. Most of us will never realize all that we are capable of because we will never be met with such challenges. Thats a good thing, I suppose. But there is also something to be said of knowing just how strong a person can be when the chips are down.

I was so deeply moved by the story Yves told of a young woman named Mayelle, that I incorporated it in my latest speaking presentation *I Want, I Will, I Win*. According to his book, on January 12, 2010, Mayelle had been assigned to represent her company at a meeting in the Montana Hotel. She was to arrive promptly at 3pm and stay no longer than ninety minutes as this would be only the first of two meetings she would be a part of that day. At 4:40pm she excused herself, gathered her things and was on her way to her next location. After saying her goodbyes, she proceeded down a large concrete staircase that led to the street below.

At 4:53pm her world began to cave in around her...literally.

The earthquake was devastating. At last count, it has taken just over 300,000 lives. 300 of which were lost at the Montana Hotel. At the time, Mayelle vowed to not let herself become a statistic. As the staircase crumbled underneath her, Mayelle made a desperate leap for the sidewalk and felt one of her sandals fly off. She paid no mind to it, choosing to remain focused only on making it safely to her mother's house located just a few blocks away. Shouts of pain, fear, even death surrounded Mayelle as she concentrated on taking one step at a time. Not knowing if the very ground upon which she walked would instantly open up and swallow her, she kept her eyes peeled ahead and pictured her mother scared and alone in the home where she had been raised. What would she find if/when she finally arrived? Would her mother be alive? Would the house even be standing? Mayelle refused to let these petrifying thoughts slow her down.

After what must have seemed like an eternity, she eventually made it to the street where she had enjoyed a carefree childhood... running, laughing, and playing. She could see that many of the homes had suffered severely while others seemed to have remained intact. Fortunately, her mother's home was one of the luckier ones. Though cracking was clearly evident, it looked as if the basic foundation was still in place. She noticed the front door hanging from the frame as she reached the porch. The old, wooden floorboards sounded their familiar creaks as Mayelle cautiously entered the house. She called out for her mother while making her way through the tiny living room and then the bedroom.

Finally, visibly shaken and equally as terrified, Mayelle's mother appeared in the kitchen doorway. Broken glass and shattered trinkets surrounded them as they rushed toward each other and embraced. Each tear represented both the joy of realizing that they were together and the terror from what had just occurred. To borrow a quote from meditation *"All that was in the moment, was in the moment."*

When the two women finally found the strength to let go of each other and take inventory of the damage, Mayelle realized she was bleeding from the soul of her foot. She reached down and removed a piece of glass from just below her big toe. It was then that she remembered losing her sandal back at the hotel. She and her mother laughed at the thought of walking several city blocks with only one shoe.

Today, over two years after the earthquake, Mayelle displays the remaining sandal in her living room as a symbol of strength and determination. The shoe also serves as her daily reminder that nothing is beyond her grasp if her will is strong enough. Mayelle now works with juvenile delinquents in Haiti and shares her story as an inspiration to those with futures that may seem less than bright. Her passion is instilling a ray of optimism within these young people and letting them know that they, too, are capable of great things. Mayelle wants each young person to feel confident they can overcome the challenges that may be before them and come out the other side a winner.

I could have listened to Yves speak for hours but, as it was, our dinner had already crept into the early morning. Dinner plates had been cleared and all wine glasses stood empty. A few among us were starting to yawn. Some had long drives home. The rest were flying out early the next day. As part of the final goodbyes, everyone acknowledged that we had become better people as a result of our time spent together.

That is how I will always remember my first trip to Haiti. I'm a better person because of the time spent with young Rafael at the orphanage. I'm a better person because of the time spent washing the feet of those who needed shoes. I'm a better person because of the renewed gratitude for all I have. I'm a better person because of the time spent with people who showed me that true charity and generosity mean more than simply writing a check. Most importantly, I'm a better person for seeing firsthand that no matter what life throws at you...poverty, pain, loss, lack of hope...it is still in my own power to smile.

EPILOGUE

*Yes, there were times, I'm sure you knew. When I bit off more than I could
chew. But through it all, when there was doubt,
I ate it up and spit it out. I faced it all and I stood tall
and did it my way.*
-*My Way*, Elvis Presley

BY ALL ACCOUNTS, *FORREST Gump* was a huge Hollywood success.
It brought in over $675 million dollars at box offices worldwide. The
film collected six Academy Awards including Best Picture and, of
course, Best Actor for Tom Hanks. A perfect blend of comedy, drama,
and romance, The Library of Congress even selected this epic piece for
preservation in the United States National Film Registry based on its
"cultural significance." *Forrest Gump* is many things to many people.
But when listing its impressive achievements and endearing attributes,
one must undoubtedly include...misleading.

Director Robert Zemeckis (*Back To The Future, Polar Express*) would
never set out to send moviegoers down the wrong path. Though he is a
master of filmmaking magic and fantasy, Zemeckis, along with Hanks,
was able to develop and present a character so genuine that audiences
longed to have him over to the house for a slice of pecan pie. The
misdirection of which I speak comes not from the story itself, but rather
from a particular quote that has become a part of Americana since we
first heard Forrest utter it back in 1994.

*"My momma always said life was like a box of chocolates. You never know
what you're gonna get."*

It is a charming and catchy quote. At first listen it seems to make
perfect sense, but realistically there is not a grain of truth to it. Life
is *nothing* like a box of chocolates. In the time you and I have spent
together through your reading of this book, I've shared some stories
with you that have not tasted very good going down and were certainly
difficult for me to swallow. Chocolate, on the other hand, *always* tastes
good. We've discussed how life constantly presents us with new and
exciting opportunities. Even those moments that are initially perceived
as challenges hold valuable lessons for us to learn. If life really was like
a box of chocolates, we'd need to look no further than the underside

of the lid to see a detailed layout of what awaits us. Never would we need to suffer the unfortunate displeasure of making a bad decision or missing a key opportunity. If you pay attention and keep your eyes open you *absolutely* know what you're gonna get with a box of chocolates. Mistaking a strawberry cream for a delicious cashew cluster only happens in the absence of focus. Life should be so simple.

You've noticed that I take a different approach in my attempt to inspire you to achieve your own personal greatness. I firmly believe the days of the traditional motivational speaker are behind us. Experimentation and example are far more effective. I am by no means a perfect man. No such man exists, as far as I am aware. There are certainly men who are wealthier, better looking, more successful, less stressed, kinder, more generous, and more tolerant than I. I won't dispute that. There are men who are able to spend more time with their children than I am, but there is no man who loves his kids more than I love mine. I wear that title belt proudly. If such a score were able to be tallied, I'm sure we could uncover men who have made fewer mistakes and more productive choices than I have. I salute them. I am not here to win any medals. I simply set out to share what has worked for *me* on my road in hopes that you will find something that works for *you* as you travel along yours.

As I wrote early on, you will never, no matter how long and hard you may search, find one book that will give you the secret to success and fulfillment. The keys to both are already inside of you. This book is the light illuminating the keyhole so that you might unlock the life you've always wished for.

As human beings, we will have incredible highs throughout our lives. We will stand on mountain tops and shout *"I'm king of the world!"* We will receive awards, job promotions, and pats on the back. There will be times where we feel nine feet tall and bulletproof. We will have moments where we laugh until we can't breathe and moments so pure and beautiful we simply stand in awe. These are your moments to savor and they are all indications of just how divine life truly is. For me, these moments are what define the word 'success.'

There are also going to be moments along the journey that are capable of bringing you to your knees. Loneliness, rejection, anger, envy, fear, loss, and a lack of appreciation are all feelings that will drop you like a sack of potatoes if you choose to let them. When I was a kid, my parents would often take us on weekend trips to Branson, MO. One of my favorite things to do, besides riding the go karts, was seeing *The Shepard of the Hills* play.

Accepting the Daytime Emmy Award for
Outstanding Game Show Host. 2012.

Based on Harold Bell Wright's classic 1907 novel, the pageant features a character named Lem Wheeler. Lem is an old hillbilly filled with Ozark wisdom. Something he said in the play regarding life's peaks and valleys has stuck with me since I first heard it as a young boy. *"A man would just naturally wear himself plumb out walking on level ground without any downhill to spell him."* Personally, I interpret that to mean we all need some rough patches to allow us to better appreciate the good times.

How many highs and lows we will have throughout our lives, and their extremes, is determined by the choices we make. Not only physical choices, but also the internal choices, our thoughts and emotions. What you think has a direct impact on how you behave. How you behave impacts the things and the people that come your way. It won't all be candy canes and ice cream floats. Successful, happy people realize this early on. The sooner you understand the power you have over your world, the sooner that sense of fulfillment will come your way. The sooner you realize there is always something to be gained from every situation, the sooner you will lose the fear and anxiety of the unknown. The sooner you take the time to invest in yourself through learning and development, the sooner you will begin to finally piece together this puzzle we call life.

A radio DJ friend of mine, the late Jimmy Paige "The Nighttime Rage," once told me that life is just one big game. The winners are the ones who learn how to play it rather than letting it play you. Though the rules are constantly changing, games happen to be my life. They are what I do and what I love. Maybe that's true for you, as well. I encourage you to not settle for just being a player. Be a winner. It's time for you to step into the Bonus Round.

I wish you all green lights...

ACKNOWLEDGEMENTS

A VERY SPECIAL THANK you to my mother and father, Jim and Anne Newton, for being the parents every child should be so lucky to have. I love you both. My thanks also to Marki Costello of CMEG, Nicole Taylor, Curt Sharp, Sean Perry, Ken Botelho, Richard Lawrence, Lee Masters, Dan Gibson, Jim Greenwald, and Alice Ross for seeing what, at the time, only I knew was inside of me and allowing me to share it with the world.

A special word of gratitude to Sande Stewart, Bob Barker, Andy Felsher, Syd Vinnedge, Bob Boden, Kevin Belinkoff, and Marty Pasetta for your inspiration and guidance that has contributed so very much to my career.

Finally, to the game show fans across the country who have been so kind as to allow me into your living rooms for so many years. Saying 'Thank You' is not saying nearly enough.